DORIS GRAF

SPIRITUALITY in Everyday Life and the ART of Living

novum pro

www.novumpublishing.com

Bibliographical data of the German National Library:

The German National Library records this publication in the German National Bibliography. Detailed bibliographical data are available via Internet under http://www.d-nb.de.

All rights of distribution, also through movies, radio and television, photo-mechanical reproduction, sound carrier, electronic medium and reprinting in excerpts are reserved.

© 2014 novum publishing gmbh

ISBN 978-3-99038-526-5
Cover Image: Doris Graf
Coverdesign, Layout & Type: novum publishing gmbh
Images: Doris Graf (32)
Translated from German into English by Globale-Kommunikation,
Owner: Peter Rudolph

Printed in the European Union on eco-friendly, chlorine-free and acid-free bleached paper.

www.novumpublishing.com

Table of content

Introduction 8
What Awareness Do We Want to Live in? 12
Receiving Light/Increasing Energy 14
Living with Dark, Heavy Energies 17
Spiritual Guidance 20
Living Joy 24
Love 28
Heaviness in Body and Spirit 30
Phases of Ending or Continuing Love/Being
and Dying/Dying and Being 32
Sexuality 36
Illness and Pain 38
Responsibility 40
Guidance 42
Ending 44
Forgiveness 48
Perceiving Energies 52
The Ending of a Relationship, Destiny? 54
The Higher Self 58
Searching – Finding 60
Final End of a Relationship 62
Trustingly Opening Oneself 64
Being Engaged 66
Recognizing the Right Path/Guidance 70
Present/Past/Future 74
Life 76
Being Tired of Life 77
Why Don't We Change Unsatisfying Circumstances? 78
Perfection 80
Hard Times in Life 81

Connecting to the Divine Level	84
Accepting	88
Adopted Patterns	89
Soaking up Life Energy	92
Balancing the Energetic System	94
Addict Behavior	96
Recognizing What Is Right	100
Advanced Consciousness	101
Living in the Moment	104
Expressing Desires	106
Integrating Energies	108
Cleansing the Energy System	109
Awakening the Third Eye	110
Healing	112
Breathing Light and Color	113
Trusting	116
Creating Energy	118
Going into the Void	119
The Lightness of Being and Assuming Responsibility	122
Demons in the Form of Addictions	123
Fate	126
Removing Blockages with Christ Energy	127
Keep Trusting	130
Dark Times	131
Interpreting Signs	134
Trapped in Circumstances	135
Hopelessness	136
Helping Others	137
The Art of Living	140
Being in the Flow	141
Love Comes, Love Goes	142
Trusting and Trusting Once More	146
Expanding Time	148
Losing the Center	150
The End of a Relationship	151

Conclusion 152
List of Exercises 153
List of Images 154
Glossary 156

Introduction

In this book I explain how spirituality can be lived in everyday life, based on my own experiences. In each chapter I discuss the key issues and, in parallel, support and promote the process and the lessons with my paintings and appropriate exercises. In this way we can approach the light and live true happiness, combined with spirituality, in everyday life.

I will explain the relationship between theory and practice in everyday life. Spirituality when lived in everyday life is a great source of enrichment. The reader is provided with "recipes" that can be used depending on their life situation. These can serve as a guide or simply as support for living. In the end, may everyone find their own purpose and the path that is destined for them.

The individual chapters and the exercises are intended to help better understand certain circumstances, support facing life, and achieve more personal harmony. The many stages of life polish us like diamonds until all of our abilities can finally shine through. If we are able to see both sides of everything (whether apparently positive as well as negative) and recognize the lesson contained for us within, we can let this awareness guide us. May life be accompanied by an abundance of power, strength and courage, so that we can come closer to the light and our destiny – as an individual and as a group – and may the consciousness of Beings of Light be increasingly attained.

For a basic understanding, my primary aim what spirituality is about. Spirituality is about the spirit. When practiced, that means that spirit exists in everything we do. Depending on our purity, we are able to allow more or less spirit to flow into everyday activities. Everyday life without spirituality, i.e., spirit, means living on a very material level where the light, and the lightness of being are lost. We feel heavy and alone instead of embraced. Connection with spirituality brings light and lightness to our existence. Our task in this life is to absorb as much spirit as possible and to let it flow through us, so that we become Beings of Light. Then we can live our destiny without becoming sidetracked, and come closer and closer to the eternal light. We were Beings of Light and are Beings of Light. As soon as we have more spirit and consciousness for our own path, life grows easier, finally becoming a dance with the universe. The path is long and at times requires patience. But once certain insights have been made, our own awareness can be used to discriminate between those things that serve the path of light and those that don't. These lessons can be repeated endlessly until they are internalized and we have attained a bit of consciousness. As soon as there is enough consciousness, we then have our own system that guides us like a compass toward the path as the goal. To then walk that path, however, requires a lot of trust, and we must be free from our minds, which continually put stumbling blocks on our path with their probing questions. We ourselves determine the world we live in. The existing consciousness, and the application of the insights won there shape the world. It is also important on our path to free ourselves from entanglements, patterns and beliefs. We should trust in who we are or in who we should be. But it is reassuring to know that everything that surrounds us is a part of our self and a reflection of who we are. Whether for good or supposedly bad, we open our eyes and recognize our path, our lesson. To recognize the signals that exist, we must also be mindful. The more aware we are, the better we understand how to interpret everything that is around us. Until we have arrived at that state, we can always turn to our helpers who will be accompanying us for a bit on our path. These helpers are from the spiritual and physical worlds. On the physical plane, they are people who have already learned this lesson and pass along their experiences to show the way. Every life has lessons waiting for us. We can always ask the spiritual helpers (e.g., spirit guides) for advice, and they are happy to help.

How long we choose to stay with a lesson is our own choice. Nobody forces us to go on. Some of us find it easier to hold onto the old and familiar, instead of allowing the unknown and the new to enter life. This part of the process is often accompanied by a fear of letting go. Often we will need help from the outside, which we should gladly accept. It is comforting to know that we can neither make a wrong choice nor choose the wrong life. It is always our path. We alone determine when we want to continue, and that's good. The responsibility lies within each of us. This does not mean that after a lesson has been competed, life becomes easier. The spiritual world has its own laws – as does the physical world. With each step forward more responsibility is demanded. Similarly, the tasks of a primary school student, because of the different level of ability, are different from those a university student must accomplish. But don't worry; as the tasks become greater on each level of your path, so in parallel will be the harvest on both the material and the spiritual planes. But it is important to recognize that material success without spiritual insight does not bring us closer to the light, and sustainable happiness does not lie solely in the satisfaction of physical needs. On the contrary, these may further entangle us with the physical world and dazzle us with their brilliance, so that we lose sight of the true light. Combining and joining the two worlds (physical and spiritual) is important. A life of spirituality without physical realization also does not bring the enlightenment longed for. Sometimes, before both poles have become unified, we put our focus onto one or the other world. That is part of the path. However, true happiness and liberation comes with their unification. This cannot be forced, either. Every lesson skipped will catch up with us and lead us back to our path. But know: the universe shows us the way and accompanies us with the help of our earthly and spiritual helpers. May we practice calmness and have the certainty that everything arrives at the right time. Everything in life has its light and its shadow for as long as we live in the duality of the physical world. The only thing we can do is to be mindful, to recognize the signs, and try to give our best in every situation. Let us approach our life and our lessons with joy. Let us be happy that we are students and are permitted to develop, and that here on earth we are already able to experience the eternal light.

At this point, I would like to thank everyone who has accompanied and supported me on my journey so far and has contributed to the creation of this book. For the sake of clarity and ease of reading, at times I use only the male pronoun. Of course, the female pronoun applies to all terms as well.

What Awareness Do We Want to Live in?

It is our choice what awareness we choose to live in. Depending on experience and character, we live with a consciousness we are comfortable with, and we attract life circumstances that make us happy or not. If we decide that we want to change them, it can be possible by releasing blockages to change our life. There are different methods for achieving this. Everything is stored in our bodies, in our spirits, and in our souls. Depending on the blockage, we have one or another filter on our perceptions, and we feel happy or not. This filter, however, can be changed because it exists only in us. It acts as a lens through which we perceive our lives. If we change our perception, we can see through a different lens, and life appears to us in a different light. Our circumstances and the people around us match up with our filter. If we want to change something in our lives, it is best to begin with ourselves. This conscious decision allows us to align ourselves with change. We have made the first step towards change. But we should also be aware that this filter provides us with safety. By changing this filter, we will also have to let go of parts of our lives and walk new paths. But it offers new opportunities and, above all, we will be able to live a more fulfilling life, in greater harmony. Together with our altered self, people and circumstances may change correspondingly and remain parts of our environment. The next step in implementing our task will be to attract the method best for us to changing our blockages, our patterns. We must also allow for sufficient time so that the changes within us can be made without pressure. We go through a process in which we can anticipate neither the time nor the result. But in any case, the effort is worth making. It brings us into a better flow and thus closer to a more fulfilling and harmonious life. Let us approach this process with joy and give our environment and our fellow human beings the opportunity to also change through our new behavior.

Receiving Light/Increasing Energy

In order to be able to communicate with spiritual beings and the dead, our energy must be increased. However, it should not be forced. Spiritual beings can be called upon and asked for help. They are capable of adapting to our energy and working with us, so we can reach the next level of energy. They can be our helpers when we ask for their help. But sometimes we need a physical helper who can provide us with valuable support for this step until we have obtained the necessary consciousness to allow us to continue on the path on our own.

In order to make contact with the dead, our awareness must already be expanded. In general, the dead can communicate only on their spiritual level, and we on ours. We do not have a connection with them, since the difference in energies is too large. But if we already have the necessary awareness, the dead can get in touch with us. In such moments, our system is capable of automatically increasing the energy so that contact can be established. However, we should not force it nor should we disturb the peace and the path of the deceased. But sometimes they want to communicate something to those left behind in the physical world. They also want to support us so we can better walk on our path. In love relationships in which one partner has left, the presence of the deceased can bring comfort and support to the bereaved. Those left behind may perceive this consciously or subconsciously, and it may help them to better overcome the period of mourning. Love does not die with the decay of the physical body. There is just a transformation into the spiritual plane. The more awareness partners have, the better the connection and perception of energy from the spiritual world can be. If a person had an expanded level of consciousness before death, the perception of the energy will not be much different than it was in physical life. But it is important to adjust the body to the respective demands of life and not always live in the same level of consciousness.

Contact with the spiritual world is not always needed and therefore our system can just as well be situated on a physical plane for the daily tasks of the physical world. Recognizing and acting on these different planes is very important, otherwise our daily lives would be disrupted and we would no longer be able to handle the tasks assigned to us; we would be out there too much. The tasks on this earth must be fulfilled and the expectations of daily life met. The better we are rooted in the earth, the more we can develop our spiritual awareness. The levels of the intellect and emotions should also be used as tools. The spiritual world can be included as an extra dimension that shows us the way to our final destination, and enables us to live a piece of paradise already here on earth. Everything in its time. The art is finding a balance between the different levels. Our body is our instrument that contains a greater or lesser amount of energy from the spiritual plane, depending on its constitution. The energy level is manifested in the human energy centers. These energy centers support each other and, ideally, are pulsing, interconnected centers. Their energy levels can be elevated by targeted exercises: with Yoga, Tai Chi and several other methods. It is up to us to find the approach right for us, and to practice it.

The power of thoughts and words must also not be underestimated. Constant negative thinking and communicating affect our entire energy system, and with time, our body will become ill. To resolve negative thinking or communicating, the underlying pattern must be recognized. But as long as we harbor and express negative thoughts, we must work at resolving the pattern so we won't become ill. The greater our awareness is, the better we can perceive the way our thoughts and words affect others and ourselves. We can also distinguish whether certain words are necessary, even if they are not harmonious. Sometimes we assume the role of serving as a mirror for our fellow human beings, so that they in turn can understand the impact of their actions. With greater awareness, however, we should be able to recognize the instances in which we serve as a mirror, and if we want to assume this role, live it consciously. This has to do with the resonance we perceive – once we are on the level of empathy. In many cases, people attract each other based on exactly this principle of resonance. Everyone assumes the role that helps them recognize his or her patterns, but in the complementary role – just as there is no perpetrator without a victim. Here too, it is important to consciously recognize your part and work on it. It makes a difference whether one willingly goes into this resonance, or participates in complete unawareness.

Living with Dark, Heavy Energies

Certain situations and certain people create a heavy energy level. The light disappears, and we are on a level of heaviness, darkness, and thoughts filled with melancholy. These thoughts are nourished by the dark level. Situations filled with this heavy energy are attracted. We feel dull, lacking in energy, and our life becomes an uphill battle. All lightness is gone. In situations like these, it is important to remember that we should surround ourselves with light things in order to overcome this heaviness. Nature can be a great helper to us here. We can also consciously fill ourselves with light so that the heaviness and darkness gives way, which can even affect our body: there seems to be pressure everywhere and sometimes even physical pain. An appropriate light exercise can be done as follows:

We sit or lie in a place that is as quiet as possible. We close our eyes and focus our mind on slowly, with every inhalation, absorbing light from the universe above by opening our upper cranium (crown chakra) and letting this light with all its rays travel first through our head, slowly through our upper body, arms, lower body and legs and, at exhalation, through the entire body. Feel how we are becoming one with this light more and more, and how lightness slowly spreads in us. Let our bodies feel and determine how much light is needed until we can feel light and free again. Perhaps we take a break by breathing calmly. If we feel we haven't absorbed enough light, we repeat the exercise. It is important to perceive the body with awareness. Where are any remaining heavy and dark places? The universe holds infinite amounts of light ready for us. Let us also feel peacefulness spread through our spirit. We repeat this exercise as often as we feel the need. Over time, the body will become accustomed to this lightness and also more resistant to falling from this higher energy level. The body becomes adapted to this energy level. All of life will orientate more towards light. More events and situations that are light will also be attracted. With more practice, the location, the stillness, and closing the eyes will no longer be that important.

I hope that you can experience much light and joy with this exercise. More enlightening beings from the spiritual world may also be attracted.

Spiritual Guidance

We have the opportunity to call on our spiritual leaders when we have problems, or even only questions, and in situations where we need assistance. Everyone can go deep inside and begin this invocation. Over time we will know whether our leaders are male or female; but ultimately, their gender is not important. It is important that we talk to them and share with them our expectations. From my years of experience, I have found that he or she is always there to provide us with support and help. In very difficult situations, spiritual guides and God can be called upon for Divine guidance. Of course, we can always pray. The invocation of our spirit guide is independent of religious affiliation: the Divine is on the highest hierarchical level. It does depend on our religion whether we call the Divine, for example, God or Allah. Because all knowledge exists on the spiritual plane, and every person is guided by a Divine plan, this knowledge is accessible at any time. The spiritual leaders are the bridge between the material physical and the spiritual world. Thanks to Divine influence, with its help, we are able to find the best possible solution for an issue or a problem. This is particularly the case when we look at the bigger picture.

From the physical point of view, we usually see just the current situation, which may seem to require a different solution, because we cannot see the big picture. A great level of trust is asked of us when we put to practice Divine impulses that may not always appear logical to us. The more often we consult the Divine, the more clearly we can see that the Divine impulses were valuable and the solutions were right – when seen over a longer period of time. Ultimately, in our highest configuration, we are also divine. But as long as we have a body, we are also human, which doesn't always make life easy. Every ambition wants to be gratified. The body wants to be nourished and its other needs addressed, such as breathing, sleeping and so on. In this world, it is about living the Divine, i.e., flowing with everyday life and giving a meaningful direction to actions. If we were to focus only on our physical needs, the Divine would come up short. We would become dull and heavy with time, and gravity would pull us down. The Divine in us lets us become bright and light and aspire to higher things. But without roots and grounding, we cannot actually live this or give form to the Divine. Therefore, we are challenged with being rooted in this world and, at the same time, opening ourselves to the Divine. With this focus, we increasingly become Divine beings with inner clarity that allows us to approach the state of paradise and live it. In the overall plan, the Divine tasks are different for each of us. If we develop according to the plan and follow it, we will achieve our destiny. Sometimes dark and difficult times are necessary for our own growth and that of others. The goal of the soul is to grow. Sometimes a dark state over several lives is required. How long we need in order to move forward with the plan designed for us by the Divine depends entirely on our own free will. In this sense, we are always on the right path and always surrounded by the right people and the right circumstances. By being human, we are often unable to consider all factors involved in problems and in making decisions. Then, Divine guidance can be a great support to us, so that we can complete our Divine plan in the best possible way. The Divine assessment is subject to laws different from those on earth and in the various cultures. This means that everyone is treated the same. A life filled with many worldly achievements is not automatically considered successful from a spiritual point of view. After our death we can't take material things with us. The higher development of man is based on spiritual values, which can be experienced regardless of the state in this world. But worldly values do not exclude spiritual ones. It is important to recognize that we should not identify with the values of the world. This would prevent the Divine alignment. Once we neglect and even forget our Divine path so we can satisfy worldly needs, we increasingly become matter, which will then dominate us as time goes by. The art is to be in this world but not of this world. True happiness and paradise lies in our divinity. But we choose the values we align ourselves with. In summary, it can be said that we should follow our Divine plan, regardless of whether this brings worldly wealth or poverty; the underlying lessons to be learned are important so that we can grow to be Divine.

We can ask our spiritual guides direct questions when we contact them. When beginners first establish contact, they may need to lie down in a quiet place so they can talk to the spiritual guides and ask them questions. Over time, their answers can be distinguished from one's own thoughts. In difficult situations, we can at any time request that our guides manifest the best possible solution. Over time, we will find that we can trust this spiritual guidance. The name we give this guidance is not relevant. But the light and not the dark should be called.

Living Joy

It is very important to express and live in joy. Sometimes, a lightness of being effortlessly develops. Strength for periods marked by painful lessons comes from these times. This level can be compared to the state of paradise. Problems are far away, and we can enjoy life to the fullest. If we want to be independent of outer circumstances, we can internalize this state and conjure it up at any time. This state of being is present everywhere. But often our circular thoughts, which have us constantly dealing with problems and possible solutions, prevent us from being free and happy. If we can learn to recall and enter this state at any time, our body and mind can relax much better. But this letting go also requires trust that ultimately there is a Divine plan. Therefore, let us let go of worries and concentrate on things and situations that bring happiness. Let small things make us happy. If we can accomplish that, we also won't be pulled down by unfulfilled expectations. We learn to recognize the good things in life more and more. Our focus changes with time more and more and we can absorb, and feel, more joy. Let us decide here and now to live in joy and happiness and to remain in that state. Every day life passes by a little more and we inevitably approach the point of death, which causes a transition and letting go of the physical body. But up to this point, we can decide whether we want to live plagued with sorrow or joyfully. Every life has times with light that let us regain strength. Let us release more and more of the thoughts that prevent us from living in joy. Let us become independent of life circumstances. The spirit is above matter. Thus, it is up to us to focus and nurture our spirits. Think of your spirit as a garden that needs care. Let us pull the weeds so that the beautiful flowers can blossom, and our garden can become a source of nourishment for our surroundings. Let good energies flow and connect with the light, so that the heaviness and darkness falls away from us and we can even pierce the darkness with our light. Let us decide today to live a life filled with joy and happiness. If we are unfamiliar with this state, we can become afraid, because the unknown can create fear. Paradoxically, clinging to familiar patterns gives us a feeling of comfort. Let us learn to recognize and let go of these patterns, so we can experience lasting joy and happiness and the seeds we planted in our garden can unfold like flowers. Let us become aware that we are Divine beings and strive towards the light in alignment with the Divine plan. To get there, however, we must resolve the darkness before the light bit by bit, so that we can let the clouds pass by and let the light shine through our lives like the sun. Everything that surrounds us in the outside world is a mirror that shows the way. Let us learn and recognize the underlying principles of life. Life is wonderful. Don't get bogged down. Let's elevate our spirits. Let us spread our spiritual wings and become inspired. Let's walk through life with inspiration.

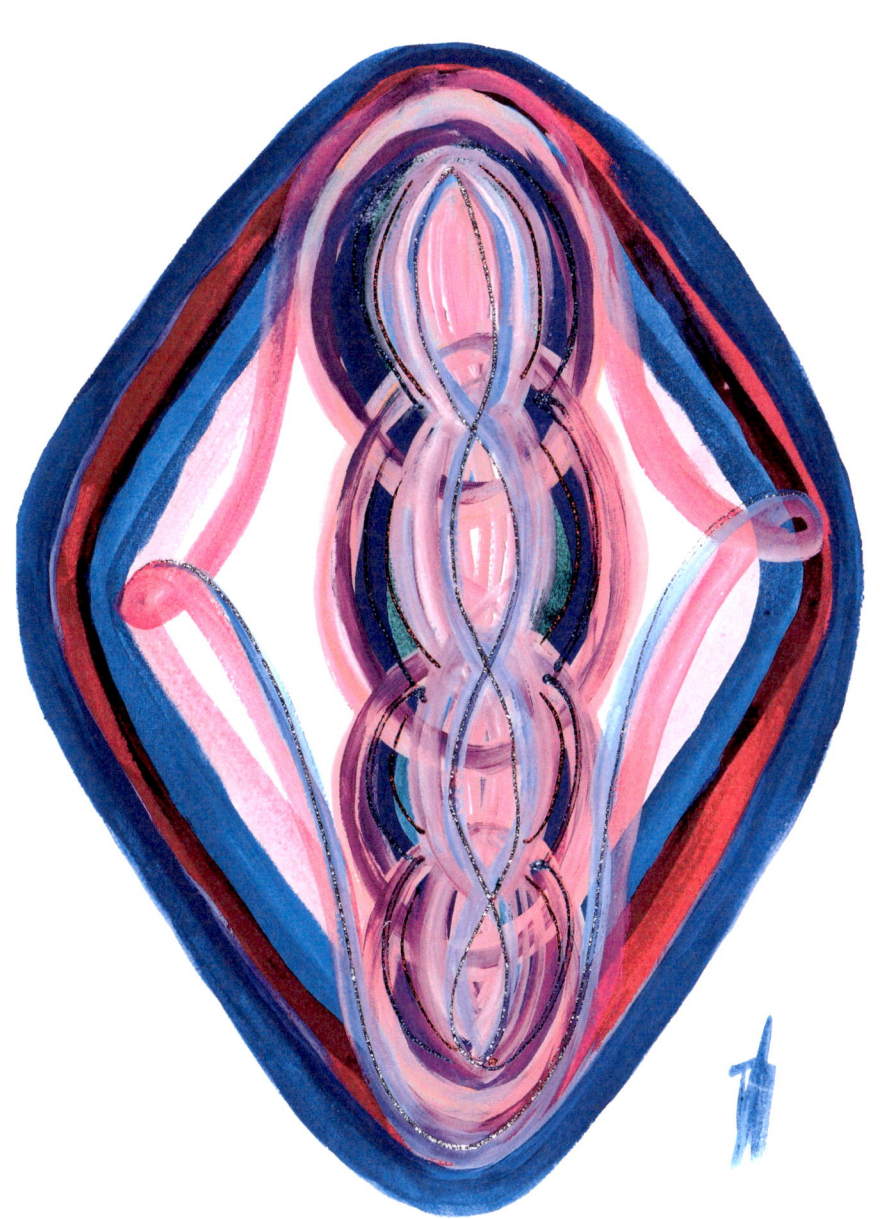

Love

Love is born out of the soul's desire to grow. Love has its own energetic potential. Love comes and goes. Love cannot be captured. If love did not exist, we would not want to engage with personalities different from our own. Love connects people who would never find each other if there were no love. Love cannot be explained by the mind. When there is love, it can be described as a magical moment. In those moments, the soul is speaking to another soul in its own language that can be understood only by these two people. Love is the strongest of powers. Love can make the impossible possible. It allows people to grow beyond themselves. Love always contains a beginning and an ending within – just like any other living thing on this earth. In the spiritual world, love has neither boundaries nor a physical body. Love knows no distance. The power of love can be directed anywhere and radiated everywhere. It is a strong and clear force. Each love has an energy potential that wants to be lived correspondingly. Even if a person fights love, it will not go away. It is within everyone's power to decide for or against love. Love is everywhere, and yet on the physical plane we cannot love all people the same. The purer and clearer we are in our development, the purer and clearer our love. Love demands devotion to love itself. Love can also cause fear when the sense of devotion equates with losing one's own self. Devotion is not the same as losing oneself. It is everybody's job to be true to themselves and their needs, even in the face of love. Over time, if love is accommodated to the point of self-abandonment, feelings of hatred are fostered, which present the negative side of love. Love's shadow is hate. This emotion can contain the destruction of one's self and others.

Love develops and nurtures itself and the beloved's growth. Caring for love, like tending a garden, preventing weeds from destroying the blossoms, is therefore essential. This means expressing one's emotions and not suppressing pent-up feelings out of cowardice and consideration for the partner. Love has many different shades and continuously challenges us to express ourselves in new ways. The love between two people has its own melody and rhythm. It is important to discover the color of this melody and its rhythm. Is a lot of or less closeness best? Is the love stormy or rather quiet? These melodies and rhythms can change over time. A love lived changes us in the long-term and provides the opportunity for growth and integration of new parts of ourselves. Love is magnificent and unique and cannot be projected onto another person. Love makes the impossible possible and gives us wings. Let us enjoy this feeling of clarity that enchants us at the beginning of a love affair, which – even after the first phase is over and the view through rose-colored glasses has faded – always flares anew. This can happen only if we are able to continue meeting each other on new levels and are willing to grow.

Heaviness in Body and Spirit

When we feel low in energy and our body and spirit are sluggish and heavy, we can actively charge ourselves with energy and light. We focus on the point at the base of the spine (root chakra). Then we visualize a fountain whose source is in this root chakra. We let beams of energy rise from this point – like water from a fountain. First, we let the rays rise to the middle of the back, then higher and higher, until the rays pour as an arch over our heads. We continue this exercise until we feel that we are light and energetic once more. We remain in this state of lightness until we have truly internalized this feeling, and our body and spirit are filled with this lightness. We breathe completely calmly, and our consciousness is entirely connected to our body. If necessary, we can perform this exercise anytime, anywhere, to raise our energy level. This is a wonderful way to become quickly filled with lightness and energy again. It is important that we direct our awareness to this exercise. The feeling of happiness is dependent on the energy level we live. As soon as we load our spirits with heavy and distressing thoughts, we can feel how our energy level decreases and we become heavy and powerless. It is therefore advisable to let go of oppressive thoughts as much as possible. Creative solutions can also be found faster and better in a state of lightness. In addition, we feel embedded in this source of energy that is available to us from everywhere in the universe. Let us become aware of the Being of Light within us. We are this light and we can live this light. It is even our duty to walk in the light rather than in the darkness. Once there is more light within us, we can also influence our surroundings with this light. People around us can feel this light and want to be near us and feel good around us. Everything on this earth is striving for light and for increasing energy. Without light there is no growth. We can develop faster and move forward on the way to light with more joy. We are Beings of Light and have the task of developing our consciousness to come to this realization. The exercise will make it easier for us to align our bodies and minds to this light, and to identify ourselves with the light of consciousness. Let us rely on our senses and do this exercise whenever we have the need.

Phases of Ending or Continuing Love/Being and Dying/Dying and Being

When love ends, the mind usually kicks in beforehand and analyzes the relationship with razor-sharp clarity. Love's shine fades, leaving behind only analysis with which the partner is mercilessly examined under the microscope. What seemed glorious before now seems to us only inappropriate and bad. From this position, we can generally no longer understand why we had given our heart to this person. It is painful to separate the connection, because the relationship connects our energy centers. The more sudden a separation occurs, the more painful the splitting of these energetic bands can be. If the relationship broke apart slowly, the final step is perceived only as a physical enactment. This hurts a lot less. And if a new relationship already exists, separation will no longer trigger pain. The successive separation of the chakras beforehand has created space for another partner, and the threads have already connected with the new person.

Why do relationships break apart? If we assume that the purpose of relationships is in furthering our development, the relationship is no longer required after the learning process is completed. But it is also possible for the relationship to take us to a next level and to further our development. This is the ideal situation. If we compare the relationship with an onion, we will always discover new levels that need to be recognized and integrated. However, both partners must engage on this new level, otherwise they must separate. Many couples remain on a level that has become lifeless and thereby impede each other's development. This lifeless level freezes the energy and eventually paralyzes both partners personality development. Instead of a lively interaction, both sides live established patterns; like a theater play that is repeated over and over and is already completely worn out. However, both cling to it. Neither can move forward. If one of the partners breaks away, the whole relationship is called into question, and the other partner attempts to bring the escapee back to the accustomed level by all possible means. Typically in such a case, an ending is unavoidable. Often, one of the partners falls in love with someone else, so that everyone can continue to live on their level; one partner experiences life on a new level and the other partner lives on the old level. Here, too, we can make the decision for or against the development. To further develop in the same relationship, both partners must be in agreement. This is in contrast to our personal choices about the extent we want to develop or not. The same is true for everyone around us. During a phase of developing, some people disappear and new people enter our lives. This is the flow of living and dying, which we can also readily observe in nature. In a bigger sense, we can also see this in the process of developing and dying. The physical form is replaced by a new, spiritual one. The less we resist the flow, the less pain we feel, and life can carry out its rhythm. This process is the same in our relationship. It shows us that we must always be ready for this process of death and development even in a current relationship, so that flow and vitality can continue and we do not become bound in lifeless suspension. Otherwise, we would be spiritually dead already in this lifetime and exist only as a physical shell.

Sexuality

The strongest union between two people on the physical plane is through sexuality. The merging of energies creates a third energy. Other than through sexuality, this bond of love can also be experienced between parents and children and in friendship. Sexual exchange can be superficial or be consciously experienced on a very deep level. Only with sexuality can children be created on a physical level. On a spiritual level, spiritual children can be created by mutual fertilization. By analogy, artists express their feelings and emotions through the art of writing, painting, dancing, or other forms. These arts are significantly influenced by relationships. Artistic expression is different from the interchange on the sexual level, however, because of the physical element of entering a person's body or receiving him into one's own. Whether sexuality happens on different levels depends on the partners' connection and their awareness. The bodies of the partners involved in the sexual exchange can be perceived as an instrument that can play every tone, or only high or low ones. The strongest exchange occurs when partners are engaged on all levels with great awareness. Then, sexuality can be perceived as an ever-renewing melody, moving ecstatically to ever-new heights. Orgasms can be perceived on a mental, emotional and/or physical level. They stimulate renewal in the partners and establish a deep connection so fulfilling that no additional stimulants are needed. This kind of sexuality will create feelings of closeness and depth in the partners over time. This opening-oneself has a positive effect on the whole personality and brings much satisfaction. It is also possible, however, to interact on a purely intellectual level and/or on the heart level without a physical level, which can also be very rewarding. With every inclusion of each of the three levels, however, more depth can be experienced; but the composition of the levels is important: an excess of physical energy can result in feelings of dullness and erosion over time that create a need for other means of stimulation. This exchange takes place in the lower chakras, and the partners are left with heavy energy. When heart energy is included, warmth and fulfillment is experienced. The further inclusion of mental or spiritual energy from the head chakras adds a universal level, which the partners experience as a Divine dimension. However, it is important to take time for this development. The body is a vessel that must first adapt to additional energy frequencies. For this reason, it is not safe to create an artificial opening by using stimulants; their use can result in mental confusion and physical discomfort. In addition, when the stimulant wears off, a potential for addiction may ensue, because man strives to approach the ecstatic state of divinity and wants to remain there. But for as long as we live in our physical body on this earth, we can only be permanently in the Divine state if we have great awareness. Prematurely inducing an artificial state has its price. Some cultures use stimulants selectively and in a controlled manner in rituals. This is not comparable to when they are used without awareness and only for recreational purposes. Self-development is the path to attaining the Divine goal.

In a further and more advanced stage, sexual energy can be provided to the whole universe by including the three levels: body, spirit and heart. This can be achieved more consciously by the following focusing exercise:

During the sexual union we bundle the created energy by imagining a pyramidal-shaped funnel over us during the sexual act. The created energy is then bundled through the pyramid, amplified and provided to the whole universe. The energy created may be intended for a specific positive purpose that serves the general good, or it can be sent randomly into the universe for the general good.

Illness and Pain

Illnesses force us to take a break in life. We take care of ourselves. If we neglect to do so, we are not doing justice to our task. Illness provides an opportunity for re-orientating and for understanding where changes or improvements in our lives should be made, so we can find better balance within ourselves and live in harmony. Depending on the kind of illness or pain, we can identify where changes in our lives must be made. If, for example, we suffer from stomach pain, we should ask ourselves if we have allowed too many undigested things admission. Does our shoulder hurt? Are we letting ourselves become burdened with too much? In this way, every disease is an indication as to how we can come into balance with ourselves. It is important to take these signs seriously. We should take ourselves seriously! After all, it is our body's signal to take a look. If we ignore this signal and merely take drugs so we can experience some relief for a while, we miss the chance to change something in ourselves. Our body is our friend and not our enemy.

But it is not always easy to interpret the signals. In many cases we need help from a specialist, such as from a doctor, a mental health therapist, or other helper. Administration of drugs or even surgery is essential in some cases. Yet it is still important to try reading the signals ourselves. Depending on how strongly our body's alarm bells go off, a re-orientation in life is generally called for. We can also speak to our bodies and ask what each area has to say, and how we can help, so that alarm bells are no longer necessary. Let us trust in our bodies. Patience is also always demanded from us. Let us be thankful for the signs. They are signals that bring us back into harmony and balance. Let us learn to take ourselves and our bodies seriously and communicate with it. We will lead a more fulfilling life in the longer term if we work with our body and not against it. Since we are a unit, we cannot separate ourselves from our body and suffering. Therefore, it is better to make peace with our bodies as soon as possible. Only when our body, our spirit, and our soul are in harmony, can harmony arise in us. Then we can live a full life, without shutting things out. Fortunately, we cannot separate from body, spirit, or soul. Therefore, it is important to perceive any signals from these three levels. We always attract only those lesson that we need, and for as long as it takes until we have learned them. That is why it is essential to pause from time to time and determine where we are in our lives. If we neglect to do so, we are thrown back by illness and/or pain so that we can re-align and reconcile our lives. Our task is to understand our path and also walk it. Let us gain awareness and take responsibility for our lives. A doctor, therapist, or other helper cannot replace our work. They can only support us and do their part. The rest is our challenge. Let us be happy to do something for ourselves and to further our development for the benefit of all.

Responsibility

The degree of responsibility depends on the load you are able to carry. The heavier the load you can bear, the larger the tasks that come your way. Some people bear more and others less. Strength develops with the tasks. In the end, we are one unit and contribute to a greater whole; this principle works the same as in our school system. But it is called the school of life. Everyone is part of it and has tasks to solve. What we sow, we reap. Occasionally, we see the reward. It is not always obvious. No pain, no gain, applies on this level. The spiritual pump catches up with us again. It can relate to this life or another one, and is called karma, the law of cause and effect. Therefore, it is important to listen to our guide so we can live in as much harmony as possible, recognize the tasks of daily life and avoid generating new karma. No deed goes unpunished. It is desirable though to continue on your way to the light and observe the spiritual laws. We can recognize these spiritual laws if we listen to our guides. They reveal themselves in feelings that give us lasting satisfaction. Then we are on the right path and in alignment with ourselves. That's why it's good to pause from time to time and determine where we are. What direction is our life taking? What makes us happy? How can we reach our full potential? What is the environment we move in? What circumstances have we created? Short-term happiness and living according to the principle of pleasure is not desirable. The long term is important, as is meditating on life as a whole. Living stubbornly according to one plan, however, is not beneficial either. Life and the soul have their own logic. Awareness on many levels is required. Only then are we guided toward our true destiny.

Guidance

The guidance we receive shows us the path that best supports our development. But how does this guidance reveal itself in our lives? How can we be sure that we are on the right path and are making the right decisions? Our willingness to accept and trust guidance is called for. Not just our own will can lead to fulfilling our destiny. We can perceive the guidance by listening to our intuition. If we feel attracted to something, feel energy behind it, then we can be sure that we are on the right path. This is not the same as intellectual analysis. In many cases, we cannot sufficiently explain why something attracts us. The mind can be used best for retrospective analysis. What happened in the past in comparable situations? What was the part that we played? What lessons can we learn so we won't make the same mistakes again? The degree of feeling attracted to something can be measured by the amount of energy it contains. Perhaps there are also signals from outside which guide us back to the right path. Why do we meet the same people over and over again? First we never see them and then they cross our paths all the time. We can interpret this as a sign. Maybe there is a task we have to accomplish together. Let us wake up and become aware of everything around us and within us, so that we can finally detect like radar what is important to our lives. We can be guided better the more we accept Divine guidance. Divine guidance requires perception and intuition rather than critical analytical thinking. Our minds often prevent this perception and throw us back into our limited world. It often disconnects us from our perceptions. Therefore it is important that we open up and perceive without immediately putting everything under critical review. If we trustingly open ourselves to the guidance and allow ourselves to be led, we will recognize better and more quickly what is right for us, so that our lives can develop according to our predetermined destiny. We will also feel part of a larger oneness, and begin trusting in life's patterns. Everything is connected, and we can recognize that we are not alone, but are one with the universe and connected to the Divine. Everything has an effect on the whole and is connected, in the end. Separation is caused by our intellectual perception. The mind is one of many instruments and helps us, as mentioned before, to understand and analytically structure our past. This instrument is very useful but must be used at the right time and not be confused with Divine guidance. The mind is always divisive; non-intellectual feeling with our senses allows us the all-encompassing perception. This also lets us see things as a whole that connect us, rather than divide us. Let us use the different instruments at the right time. If we live our lives with Divine guidance, we feel embedded in the whole and with time can see the meaning behind things. Divine guidance knows the overall plan of our lives and beyond, which is most commonly obscured, because we perceive only the current situation. Let us trust and submit to this Divine guidance. Our own point of view is limited by linearity of time, which resolves as soon as we open up beyond linear time and move out of the worm's-eye view. Let us follow the wonderful plan designed for our lives. Let us trust in our intuition and let our self-consciousness grow.

Ending

When something is ended, it feels like dying off. But something has to be ended first, before something new can appear in our lives. Ending can start already in a current situation. Ending is not an outward ending. In general, ending is a process deep within us that starts at a given time and continues until it is completed. In general, it involves pain. Every ending also involves dying. Something that already exists cannot develop further. The energy decreases and it is time to say good-bye. Leaving can be abrupt or proceed over an extended period of time. Sometimes we have to go through this process because of outside circumstances, either the initiative comes from the outside, or we initiate it on our own. Leaving always involves pain and a subsequent emptiness because the current energy decreases until it is finally gone. But after the pain and mourning, new opportunities await us. It is important not to shut out this opening, and to give life a new chance, to connect with new things. We approach life with new insights and experiences and see life with a broader awareness. The pain is strongest when we recognize that love is dying. All feelings of happiness and illusions about a person are followed by awakening, and disappointment sets in. Our view of things is no longer supported by the brilliance of love. We were wrong, and the initial potential of the love was not fulfilled. We invested into developing the potential and expended a lot of energy up to the point at which we recognized that our perceptions were not realized, and we can no longer shut our eyes to the reality we are presented with. Instead of the feeling of happiness, we feel emptiness that grows when the efforts for this love have been depleted. Instead of further development of love, a gradual death sets in. With every hurting and inflicting of wounds a little bit of love chips away until there is nothing left in the end. Both partners must be committed to keep love going. One partner alone cannot support the development and the love over a longer period of time. When, after hurt and disappointment, love can no longer be maintained, the time of ending has come. There is no more movement, the love has died, and the energy that used to drive the love has been depleted. With every new love and every beginning, a seed of either growth or death is planted. A third entity is created that must be nourished like a flower to grow. From time to time, weeds must be pulled. But if we approach it with lack of respect, the wrong fertilizer, then the plant, this third entity, which we have a relationship with, slowly dies. The healthy cells are depleted, and a dead structure is left behind that is not worth keeping alive. In general, we have several opportunities to nurture the structure and support its development. Therefore we should treat it carefully and with respect.

Forgiveness

Every event leaves behind its traces. Positive or negative emotions may be connected to the event. They are stored in connection with people, things or places. Their traces descend deep into our soul. Accordingly, positive or negative feelings are generated with people, things or places. If we had very bad experiences with a person, we will have negative preconceptions over time. In the opposite scenario, we will give others a bonus. It is very hard for us to separate from the past. It is our organ of perception that we rely upon over time and that guides us. This organ of perception cannot be tricked. And even when it can, only for a short time; then our memories will resurface. If too many negative experiences are associated with one person, we avoid interacting with that person. There is no more joy and the negative feelings weigh too heavily on the relationship. In most cases, the relationship ends. But often, these experiences relate back to us. We attract situation like these and play our role. We also have important experiences and can move on with our lives in a positive way with the insights gained. The experiences have a lasting effect on our attitude. But not every person who enters our life for the first time should be viewed only through the negative filter. The important thing is to recognize that we too played our role in the negative experience, and with this new insight we can now interact more maturely with our outside world and our life. If, for example, we are too trusting, we can learn to become more critical without assuming that everyone is full of good intentions in life. It is our job to keep our eyes open and learn to discriminate between good and bad. This polarity exists in this world so that we can decide how to love and which energies we want to connect with. Without this discrimination, we are helplessly at the mercy of the powers that be, and will keep letting others take advantage of us. Some people provide us with the opportunity of recognizing this. The decision is ours whether we want to stay in this environment, and how long it will take for us to learn our lesson. In that sense, there is no good or bad. Yet, in the long run, we want to feel good and not always delve in negative energies. These heavy energies are life-defying and cause illness. Often, we only learn important lessons by becoming sick and then take a new course in life. If we are aware of this, we can avoid these tough experiences. Remember that every experience relates to us. If we aren't able to recognize our role we will continue to attract similar situations. Therefore, it is generally not advisable to avoid people or situations without having learned our lesson. We can sense whether we have learned our lesson by attracting other circumstances. But it is our choice to move forward and leave people that are not good for us. Nobody forces us to stay in an impossible situation. It is more important to remember that our environment is our mirror, to look closely and see how the situation relates to us, and to work on ourselves. That's why it is important to not take everything so personally, and to recognize that the other is playing his role, too. But we can only be responsible for, and work on, ourselves. Whether the other person wants the same is up to him. And therefore, it is better for us to concentrate on our own development and on ourselves. That's the only way we can be sure to be walking on the right path. The other person does not have to change in order for us to be happy. If he is no longer in alignment with us, he won't be in our environment anymore anyway, and we will attract someone more suitable. Our soul knows this, and that is why we sometimes stay with people and persist in situations until we have learned our lesson. The important part is to focus on ourselves, and to take responsibility for our lives without feeling responsible for the actions of others. The exceptions are with children and pets, for whom we must assume responsibility, and when we assume leadership where we have made the conscious decision to take on a role of responsibility.

Perceiving Energies

How can we avoid being influenced by our outside world? Every constellation in the outer word has its own energy frequency. If we participate in a situation, we subconsciously connect with this frequency. This, in turn, triggers the corresponding energy in us. For example, we may allow the news in the media to influence us. We feel happy or sad depending on the kind of news. If we make the conscious choice to stay within our own center, we can attain a continuous state of high energy. But this requires great awareness and strong focusing on this level of energy.

How can we even recognize what this energy level, which we strive for as a constant state, feels like? All manner of meditative practices can help and support us in recognizing it. In the beginning stages of practice, it can also happen that we become more transparent and are even better able to take in everything that surrounds us. Obtaining this intermediate stage, however, should not be the final goal. Otherwise, we would be at the mercy of our surroundings, and our independence would be restricted. In further stages, we can make the conscious choice of being open to only certain perceptions. This can help those active in healing arts, for example, to consciously submerge into the patient's energy field and to support him with their consciousness. In even further stages, we come to the point of being able to cleanse and realign these energy fields if they are blocked. But this requires us to be consciously and firmly connected with the higher energies so that we don't tap into and deplete our own. Ultimately, we are merely a channel and cannot accomplish anything on our own. It is always the higher self, the Divine power, which is present in abundance and at our disposal. The focus on higher energies, and our awareness help us act as a medium for our fellow beings, and to support them on their path toward the light.

By removing blockages, set patterns are removed at the same time, causing a reaction in the person seeking help. Old memories, which have accumulated in the body, may awaken and can be consciously worked on and released. Often, these are suppressed situations, those we haven't released yet. They can cause a blockage of energy in the body, spirit, and soul and can ultimately cause disease. These blockages are further activated over and over again, because they are within our field of energy and attract the same in accordance with the law of resonance. Therefore, we are usually trapped in this pattern until we are able to become more conscious, release the blockages, and once again let the energy flow better in the energy field. Then we come closer to our Being of Light and our final destiny. We will feel ready to approach new things that correspond better to our frequency of energy. In order to remove the blockages, we generally need companions who are aware of the energy and can help us remove the blockage so we can continue on our path. Ultimately, we are all Being of Light and can complete our destiny as parts of the Divine.

The Ending of a Relationship, Destiny?

At a certain point in a relationship, energy no longer strives towards development, and it decreases. The ending, which is contained in this energy, is approaching. The lightness and the momentum of development are gone. It feels like an inner death of a once vital and uplifting feeling. Everything about the other is perceived in a negative way. Gone are all splendors that in times of love had lit up the loved one like a character out of a fairy tale. The tiniest negative traits are perceived with an exaggerated sharpness. Things now are seen in a disturbing light that we had previously generously disregarded. The delight over wanting to spend time with the loved one has disappeared. We start looking for excuses, begin setting different priorities. The other person loses importance. We are left with a feeling of staleness. How is it possible that I wasn't able to really see this person over such a long time? The veil of love is dropped. What remains is an ordinary person with all his weaknesses. Where did the love go, the excitement of looking forward to seeing the person and consuming him? How could it have come to this? With every wounding and unfair conduct, a bit of love dies off. With a great love, there is more tolerance. But even a great love can die and unravel through unjust treatment. What remains is an illusion of something that could have been. Love is a tender plant that cannot be beaten with a hammer. A third entity between two people develops right from the beginning: a stroke of luck and a godsend, allowing us access to the delights of eternity. We feel as if in paradise, are enveloped by this feeling of warmth and lightness. The whole world is cast in a rosy light. All problems are far away and life shines in all its glory. All the more love's demise leaves this shallow feeling. It involves the dying of this third entity. Could it have been prevented? Is it destiny? Is it within our control, or do we live according to a plan and meet people that are exactly appropriate? Are we actors in a play on this stage called Earth? There are lots of questions and no answers at the moment. Let us trust in destiny; that everything has a meaning, and we have to follow this path until we die so we can meet our destiny. Believing and trusting that everything in life makes sense, which we can probably recognize at a later time, is a comforting thought. Therefore, it is best to keep faith in the good things life has to offer and to remain open to everything that life has yet to send our way.

The Higher Self

What is the higher self? How do I communicate with the higher self? How can we use meditation to achieve states in which communicating with our higher self is easier? We can communicate with language, images or feelings. It is important to identify the form of communication that works best for us. If we have questions, we can simply ask them and observe in which form the response is made. This perception depends on our personal nature. Everyone has to find out for him or herself. Trust your intuition. The more often we communicate, the easier it becomes to perceive the answer. Let's be open to any form of response. We can also ask for a name of the higher self in the sense of a spiritual leader. It is important to be filled with as much light as possible at all times. Let us call upon the light, so that it can more readily access our higher selves. This energy level also elevates us to lightness and at the same time connects us with all beings that are on this level. This connection with the light strengthens our own light. It helps us to operate from a higher level and to live our lives in joy and harmony. This way we can also better reach our goals. Our higher selves, who recognize the bigger picture for us, support us and can help us achieve our higher goal. Let us learn to allow the guidance of the higher self to lead our way. Then we can experience more peacefulness and assuredness and know we are on the right path. Let us recognize every challenge in life as a chance to develop according to our destiny. Let us also learn to live in the here and now, so we can meet the demands of our current life and enjoy it. In addition to periods of activity, there are also times of conscious resting, comparable to high tide and low tide. Let us try to perceive this rhythm. We can practice the following exercise:

We sit or lie down quietly. We visualize the ocean. We perceive the sounds, the smells and the color. We feel the high and low tides. When we breathe in, we let waves wash over our bodies like a tide, starting from the feet to the head. When we exhale, we relax the whole body from the head to the feet and allow the water to recede – like the low tide. We breathe quietly and feel in our bodies. We stay in this rhythm until we have internalized the activity and passivity within. Let us learn to consciously let go and relax. As soon as we feel ready, we slowly open our eyes and move our bodies. Now we try to integrate this feeling into our lives. This balance is important so we won't exhaust ourselves and can remain active at the same time. This exercise can be repeated as often as necessary. It is an excellent relaxation exercise. We also develop a good sense for the balance between activity and passivity.

Searching – Finding

We all have dreams and envision, for example, the ideal job or the ideal relationship. When we are introduced to something new, we project our desires and ideas of what supposedly makes us happy onto this new event. We feel happy to have finally reached the desired goal. Over time, we realize that not everything is as it first seemed. We are disappointed. We were wrong and want to project our vision onto something else. We begin looking once again. This happens consciously or subconsciously. In accordance with the law of resonance, we attract only what corresponds to us. Thus, our task is to change our resonance and emit a different one. Otherwise, we will continue to attract the same and find the same shortcomings, so we either resign to it in disappointment, or turn away and look for something new. The true process would be to develop ourselves before we can attract something more harmonious. We have to first create more harmony within, so that we can be in better harmony with our surroundings and ultimately find happiness. If we look at our outside world as a mirror, we can see clearly where we have to work on ourselves. With everything that happens to us, we are provided with the opportunity of becoming a little more conscious and of perfecting ourselves. If we are still experiencing disharmony with our environment, it is time to go beyond the books and do inner work. It is not always easy to know where we need more development. In this sense, life is an exciting path, which provides us with opportunities and circumstances that allow us to get closer to ourselves and to finally experience universal harmony. Though this approach may often be rocky and long, it's worth taking so we can advance a bit further with every insight we made. If we cannot see clearly where we have to develop on our own, we can also see a specialist who can accompany us a little on the way. Do not quarrel with fate; this will not move you forward. Let's enjoy all the beautiful things we have in our lives. Let us also learn to accept the little things with gratitude and to be happy about them. Ultimately it is always about searching for and finding our inner selves. In the dual world, our surrounding is a mirror that we should gratefully accept. Every resistance costs time and energy that we could better reserve for advancing on our path, allowing us to more joyfully reach our goal: harmony within ourselves and with the world around us.

Final End of a Relationship

When is a relationship finally over? How do we know when it is time to end a relationship? As a general rule, every relationship takes its due course. A longer relationship has a larger amount of energy at the beginning. We are in love and are happy. As time goes on, we experience disenchantments that reduce the energy of the relationship and our love. No longer are we as euphoric, but now see our partner's short-comings. In the worst case, the process continues; we are disappointed over and over again, and finally we come to a point at which we feel no more love. Often, our destiny helps by letting us recognize with outside things that this relationship is no longer working and should no longer go on. Situations will arise that point to an inevitable ending. If external events like these repeat, we can assume that our so-called destiny – we can also say our helpers from the spiritual world – is pointing to the end. It is therefore important to pay attention to the signals. At a certain time an insight and a situation arrive that make an ending inevitable. How can we sense, and then know, that this moment has come? Whether the end of the relationship is brought about with our words or with external circumstances does not matter. It is clear that the end is there. But an ending always contains an opportunity for starting a new relationship that is better aligned with our developmental process.

Trustingly Opening Oneself

Life is always presenting us with situations that allow us to grow. These lessons present themselves to us whether we are open to life or not. We make life even more difficult for ourselves with a negative attitude. Life is the way it is. We can make friends with our destiny and make the best of it, or resist and swim against the stream until we must give in to our destiny anyway. It is our life, which we can welcome or can deny. But we don't have another life. We can be happy about little things or get upset about little things. To a certain point, we can decide for ourselves what the direction of our focus should be. That is why we can trustingly open up to life, even though we may not be comfortable with the lesson. Still, we can be confident that ultimately we will be in a situation that allows us to grow so that we can come closer to our destiny. This trust is sometimes difficult to maintain, especially when life puts us to a hard test. In general, there is no growth without pain. But we can open ourselves to this growth with happiness, so we have more joy. Once we trust that everything is all right, we can open ourselves to life more and be less worried about the future. It might require several experiences to achieve this level of trust.

Being Engaged

When we open ourselves, we take in many impressions around us. What do we do with these sensations? Do we engage with what we see? When we open up, something wonderful happens. We connect with our environment on different levels. We are aware of channels other than those our five senses provide us. To engage with our sensations requires a lot of trust in taking our perceptions seriously, and not dismissing them as mere fantasies. It is a wonderful tool that helps us gain a broader view. But in order to apply in a really practical way what we perceive, it is important to observe and reflect on whether our perceptions are also useful. The better we know ourselves, the better we can discriminate between what is coming from the outside and what comes from our inner selves. Therefore, it is also very important to check our system often in phases of retreat, and return to ourselves, so that we can connect with our environment even more. The purer our system is, the more accurate our perceptions are. It is very important not to lose ourselves in tangled fantasies. That is why it is wise to keep ourselves as pure as possible. But this will happen all by itself at some stage in our development. It is not good to control our development by our will: it would only make us skip important stages that we must revisit later with painstaking work. This opening of perception is fundamentally something very valuable. But it should not lead us to manipulate others. This would ultimately mean that we would fall behind in our development and not continue to evolve in the light. Thus, opening-up should not be forced artificially, such as with use of drugs. Once we are ready to open, it will happen on its own. Opening up early has the danger that our system is not ready and thus becomes overwhelmed. We damage our system and weaken it. It is best to rely on our spiritual guide and to try to give our best in every situation. This will automatically support our development and provide us with the rewards of expanded perception. Let us trust that everything happens at the right time, and that we assume more responsibility with more power as our development progresses. As long as it is not yet time, let us enjoy our path and try not to push a developmental process for which we are not yet ready. Every phase takes its time and brings us good as well as bad for as long as we live in this world of duality. Let's show consideration and respect for our path and practice composure whatever happens. Then, our development will continue all by itself, and we will finally become Beings of Light.

Recognizing the Right Path/Guidance

A path that is right causes an attraction that points us in the right direction. Spiritual guidance is always at hand. Submitting to this guidance has nothing in common with a linear way of thinking. Intellectually, we will not be able to retrace some of our decisions in a logical way. Only in hindsight will we understand the meaning, and be able to interpret decisions and actions that before didn't appear wise. Patience is called for, and opening up to life with trust, and walking the path with joy. We may be able only later to harvest the fruits of our labor.

The same is true for the relationships we engage in. People who attract us often have the purpose of reactivating knowledge of the past and bringing awareness to us on all levels. So let us not analyze with the mind, but open ourselves to life and engage with it. Especially those people who are accustomed to working and analyzing with the mind will find this difficult, because there is no obvious logic behind it. But it is always useful to listen to your inner guidance, because we cannot see the overall picture or comprehend and interpret all aspects with minds that are rooted in the physical world. We are always asked to trust in the higher powers. We repeatedly collect evidence in the physical world that can substantiate this path. Ultimately, we will be able to expand our consciousness and gain more and more insights. Some insights, however, will be kept hidden from us until the right time has come, because we first need to gain the understanding relating to it. If we knew everything already in advance, we could not actively have experiences that make us more conscious on our path. The mind is always trying to trick us because the guidance does not always seem logical in the moment. But we are asked to disengage from the linear level and to open ourselves to the world of infinite possibilities. Let go of our minds and connect with the greater that surrounds us and also leads us. So we relax and trust in our path, which will bring harvest and perfect consciousness at the right time. If we ask for guidance, we will receive guidance. We should also thank our guides for being there for us and providing us with their assistance. Thank you!

Present/Past/Future

In the physical world, time is linear. We only see the time segments we are currently living. With an expanded perception, we can travel with our spirits into the past and future. We realize that there is a wider spectrum of realities. Current events are in part meaningless without the perspective of the past or the future. When needed, our spirit allows us to look into the past or into the future. We can ask for this and, if receiving an answer is fitting, we will be provided with this expanded view. These insights reach us via meditation or dreams. It may also be that we suddenly receive insights as part of our daily consciousness. When we connect with this infinite dimension, we live in Divine unity and can suddenly better understand all the levels and realities. But in general, it is important to listen to our intuition and follow it, even if we do not have the overall view of how things are. To live in accordance only with the mind does not further our development. Decisions that are made solely with the mind and against all feelings and inner inspiration are usually, in the long run, not the best life decisions. Let us have trust in our inspirations, even if they may not seem reasonable at the moment. This allows us to act cautiously and farseeing.

Life

What is life? Life can have many facets. From happiness to sorrow, anything is possible. We can influence our life up to a certain point, but the important things in life are predestined. We can accept this or reject it. Life offers us many things when we are open. Be open to everything that comes: to love, to the good, and to everything life has to offer. Sometimes we want to shut down, because we have lost faith in the good and don't want any more suffering in our lives. But this shutting out prevents us from living and also prevents letting the good back into our lives. Let us hold back on judgment and accept what life offers us. Sometimes life is incomprehensible, fascinating, and it may change from one moment to the next. Let us engage with life. We receive its fruits at any age. We cannot expect to always be happy: otherwise, inevitably, we will be disappointed. Basically we cannot expect anything. Everything is a gift. Therefore, it is good to be grateful for all the beautiful moments, and to enjoy them to the fullest. Happiness lies within those moments. Let us not spoil our happiness; rather let us live in the moment, whatever that may be.

Being Tired of Life

Sometimes there are situations in life in which we feel very uncomfortable; there seems to be no meaning and nothing is going the way we want. We want everything to be different. And yet it seems that we can't just sneak out of our lives. Something is holding us back. What is this something? Why can't we just change everything at once, for example, leave our job and end the relationship? We simply can't manage this. Perhaps this is coupled with nothing better being available. We feel forced to stay in this situation. It almost seems as if we have to wait for the moment in which the opportunity for change arises. It's like a disease that we cannot get rid of overnight, but have to see how it develops. Although we can go to the doctor, most often he cannot simply magic it away either. Sometimes we are forced to persevere, to wait and look for a sign that better times are coming. It sounds quite negative, as if we are forced to endure situations without making changes. Although there are indeed situations in life that we can change, there are others on our path that we simply cannot shake off. These situations call for perseverance and faith that life will show us its sunny side again.

Why Don't We Change Unsatisfying Circumstances?

A relationship doesn't work anymore. We are no longer lifted by the lightness that we originally felt. The feelings we shared are sluggish and sometimes we even feel repulsed. The magic veil of love no longer binds us together. Perhaps only one of the partners feels the connection or neither of them do. In addition, we complain about everything our partner does. The formerly positive feeling for his/her attributes and abilities is gone. We now dismiss what we previously perceived as good and attractive; it bothers us. Still, we do not let go of the partner and stay stuck in the connection. Is this the force of habit, or is there something left for us to learn? We would assume so, if we live by the principle that there is nothing around us that does not fit. Perhaps it is the beginning of the end. If we cannot let go in such situations, we should accept it and see how the whole thing develops. This unsatisfying circumstance could be our job or another area in our lives. It is important that we do not judge ourselves for not doing anything. We accept ourselves and what we live. Let us observe, and thereby recognize the signs, so we can take action when the right time has come. We may also ask for understanding and then see what happens. But this applies only when we feel incapable of taking action. Once we clearly feel the need for action, then its time has come.

Perfection

Everything is perfect just the way it is. We see shortcomings using our minds. We have our ideas of what our lives should be like. If our lives don't develop according to our expectations, we are disappointed. If we stick to our ideas, we continue to feel betrayed by life. Let's live without general preconceptions and accept that everything around us is part of us. Then we realize that everything is perfect. If we change ourselves, our life circumstances change, too. But how should we change? By not fighting the life we live, our consciousness will already change. Let us learn to look at our lives without judgment and to accept it the way it is. Then we will see ourselves relax and we can let go of our expectations. If we can go a step further and can realize that the process of changing our lives is up to us, we can begin to work on ourselves. As long as we try to change others, we will not change ourselves. Besides, trying to change others is very difficult. By looking at our life in a non-judgmental way, we also recognize areas that need development. We can then work on these areas. We can take back all the energy that we used for changing the other, and use it for working on ourselves. It is important that we learn to read our surroundings. This way we will recognize how we are living. Are we not getting the closeness and tenderness we need from our partner? How does our own sense of worth look in this regard? Do we feel that we deserve attention and affection? Then we can begin to appreciate ourselves first and satisfy our needs. This path will ultimately lead us to where we want to be. Everything we desire has its complement in ourselves. If we don't treat ourselves in a loving way, others won't either. We deserve as much as we grant ourselves inside.

Hard Times in Life

At times it appears that life is very difficult. Despite all the intellectual knowledge, there are always times of confusion. The windows of the soul are not transparent, and we are always wondering why we are in this situation in life, and why life does not develop according to our expectations. Why might that be? Doubt gnaws at us. "What is the point?" we ask ourselves. Are we really on the right path? In times like these, we must simply clench our teeth and move forward. It gets us nowhere to keep letting our thoughts go around and around. We feel unhappy and this only makes the feeling stronger. Trust our higher guidance and continue as before. If the time for change has not yet come, we would just be squandering energy and cannot change the situation to our satisfaction anyway. Let us have faith that after hard times, bright moments will follow, and we will be happier. Observe the signs from the inside and from the outside until things are clear again and the situation can be changed. Often, confusion and uncertainties such as these appear just before a life change. It is the phase of maturation. The old no longer has its full power and the new has not yet arrived. Let us stay aware and compose ourselves internally. Let us not be impatient; hasty actions will otherwise make us lose the overall picture, creating greater problems. Continue to trust and do not lose faith.

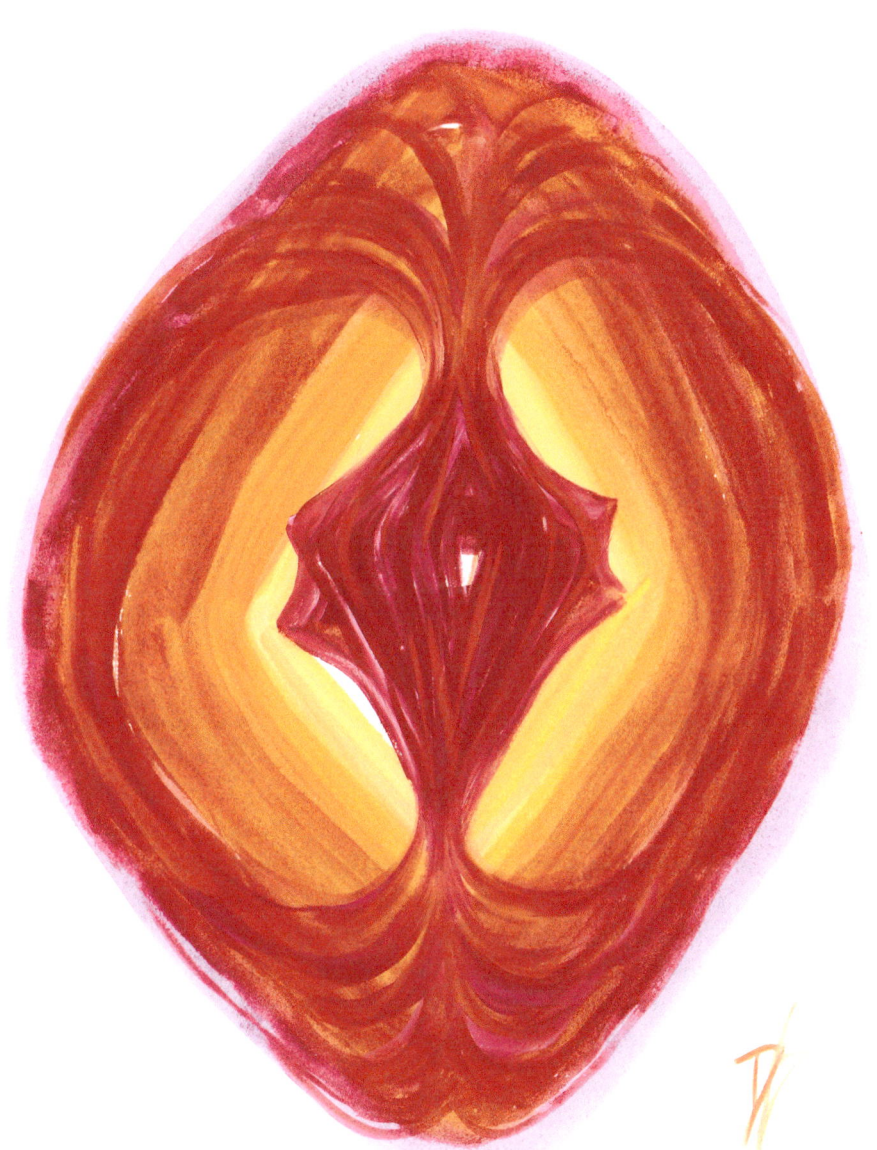

Connecting to the Divine Level

We are always surrounded by everything. The Divine level and all other levels are always present, depending on the stage we are at. Depending on our personal state, we are not always able to find access to all levels. But at higher stages of development it becomes easier to immerse oneself into the Divine level and to connect with it. This level gives us the purest energies. However, it is also good that we first develop ourselves and adapt our bodies to these energies, because they are very strong. If we succeed in reaching the Divine level with our spirit and let this energy flow through us, we will always continue to evolve. The Divine level also has its hierarchies, which – according to our developmental level – are open to us or closed. The more aware and more advanced we are, the purer the connection will be. Our spiritual perceptions will intensify and our entire system will be touched. At a certain stage in the spiritual world, we have arrived at the Divine level. This allows us to communicate only with beings of pure form. If we work in the healing arts and are connected to this world, we will be able to use this pure energy for healing. From this point on, so-called miracles may appear where the Divine is no longer limited by physical boundaries. There are laws in the Divine level that we should respect. If we fail to do so, this level will close for us again. These laws are mostly for our own protection. The further we advance, the greater the impact of our actions. For this reason, it is important to abide by the laws so that we do not misuse these powers. With each step in our development, we will learn what the level contains. At the same time, the additional gifts make other things impossible. We will also develop a purer life the further we move forward. This allows us to keep the vessel of our bodies pure as well. But this process cannot be forced. From a certain stage of development onward, the process will automatically initiate, and the necessary insights will be revealed to us. We are free to choose, and we can abide by the process or not.

Accepting

Again and again we are challenged to accept what life offers us. If everything were as we imagined it to be, we could accept life without problems. The husband or wife who does not meet our expectations, the children who do not always behave the way we expect. And yet we cannot always separate readily from the people or circumstances around us that we don't like and that don't correspond with our ideas. Actually we would like to separate, but bonds and feelings prevent us from separating. We may fight because life does not always align itself in accordance with our expectations. But fighting will only lead to frustration and ultimately to a pointless battle. It is important to recognize when we can and should make changes, and when the time is not ripe or the life situations would not change as a result anyway. What we can do is accept the situation and not allow ourselves to become depressed or discouraged. Perhaps this acceptance will suddenly facilitate completely different options. But resisting life itself and splitting off from parts or feelings of one's own self are both pointless. Eventually our lives will catch up with us. There are certain lessons we cannot escape. Our only companion is the confidence that everything that was once full will become empty and vice versa, and that life is always changing, whether we like it or not. This way we can try to be in the flow and meet the challenges we are presented with.

Adopted Patterns

As life goes on, we realize that certain behaviors always repeat. Certain situations run their course according to a certain pattern. When we suddenly become aware of this, it could be that we discover patterns inherited from childhood as the source. For example, we keep choosing partners who, from a rational point of view, appear unsuitable, and therefore we choose impossible relationships. The partner is on the other side of the globe (that does not necessarily prevent a relationship but makes it more difficult), is married, violent, or an addict. In principle, there are, at first glance, much more suitable matches in the world. Why do we look for these unsuitable ones and fall in love? Let's take a closer look at events of our childhood. Have we taken on a pattern from one of our parents? By no means is there intent to assign guilt, rather to recognize patterns we may have inherited from our parents, the people we first connected with. These do not necessarily have to be our parents if we had other primary contacts. Did we experience relationships with inappropriate partners in childhood? What is the drama we are repeating? Sometimes, with infallible certainty, we search out the relevant 'actors' with whom we can repeat our childhood drama. Often, belief systems are behind these patterns, such as: "a partner will make me unhappy or hurt me." Let us try to remember what happened in our childhood. What role did we play in the corresponding patterns and belief systems? Which energies (patterns) still remain in our system? Once we have understood, we can go into these energies and try to change them consciously. Often we need to see a specialist. But we can also try to resolve them on our own. We can practice the following exercise:

We visualize a situation in childhood where the pattern was lived. If belief patterns are the source, we always include these. Let us energetically enter into this situation. Then we visualize golden light and wrap it around ourselves. We repeat this until we feel good and everything is saturated with this energy. Then we imagine how the situation would ideally be. We visualize this and create, if need be, new, positive belief patterns. With these images, let us once again be filled with this golden energy from head to toe. This exercise should be repeated as many times as needed until we notice a change in our lives. Repeating the positive beliefs during the day and imagining how our body is permeated with this gold, and shines accordingly, can assist the process.

Soaking up Life Energy

Are we tired and feel run down? Are we susceptible to illness? This is always a sign that we are not sufficiently connected to the universal life energy. There is not enough life energy in our physical body. With the following exercise, we can raise our energy levels once again, so we can energetically handle our obligations in every day life. We can practice the following exercise:

We lie on the back and relax entirely. We become aware of our body and first let go of the feet, then the lower legs, the thighs, the buttocks, the abdomen, the belly, the chest area, fingers, forearms, upper arms, neck and head. With a deep inhalation, we focus on one body part, beginning with the feet; then we breathe out slowly and let go. Finally, our whole body is relaxed. Then we slowly inhale the color red, and visualize – if possible – the color red, filling our body with it with each inhalation. When we exhale, we release from our bodies all the old energies that do not support our life energy. We repeat this exercise until we feel that our whole body is filled with life energy. Then we lie still a little longer, feel our bodies, and get up strengthened and recharged.

Balancing the Energetic System

On a non-material level, our system is composed of energy. This energetic system has various energy centers. When the energy centers are balanced, we feel balanced and filled with energy, vitality and joy. To balance these centers, we can consciously breathe colors. This breathing is described in the following exercise.

Depending on the desired effect, the same exercise can be practiced with other colors. The additional colors, however, must be used deliberately, because they activate different energy centers (chakras) – described below – and create different energy levels. Depending on intent and effect, a different color is breathed. It is important that we are aware of our intent before breathing. For specific strengthening we can use the colors individually. For example, if we want to calm down, we breathe with the color blue. For creativity, we breathe the color green. If we want to strengthen the power of the mind, we choose the color yellow, and for a greater sense of security, the color orange. We breathe the color pink when we want to feel more love. The color violet activates spirituality. The color gold purifies our entire system and brings strong energy. This order of colors was chosen only for the purpose of example; other colors may be included which are associated to the energy centers described in the following. During breathing, it is important to observe the effects in us and to sharpen our own perception.

These color exercises can also be performed in a single exercise by focusing on the individual energy centers with their associated colors. These energy centers connect us with the energetic level. On this level, we are not aware of our physical being and we focus on this energetic level using these colors exercises. Depending on the balance or imbalance, certain colors dominate. When we focus our breath on all of the centers, we do not specifically focus on one state, but charge and harmonize our entire system with all colors. We start by first relaxing – as described in the previous exercise (chapter "Recharging Life Energy"). With focused color breathing, we visualize first the color red and breathe this color into the base of our spine (root chakra) to address our physical sensations such as pleasure or pain, and our anchoring in the physical plane. Then, we breathe the color orange, which is associated with the sacral chakra located approximately a hand's width below the navel, and is responsible for our emotional life. When we breathe the color yellow, we focus on the area that is about a hand's width above the navel (solar plexus) and is associated with the intellect (navel chakra). Next we concentrate on the color pink with a focus on the region around the heart (heart chakra), which represents our ability to love. The color green is associated to the throat area (throat chakra), which speaks to the power of the word, among others, and the blue color is associated with the space between the eyebrows (the energy center called the "Third Eye") and is responsible for perceiving the energetic level. When we breathe the color violet, we focus on our crown and activate our crown chakra, which connects us to the spiritual planes. If we focus on the centers and on the respective color breathing, we will feel for ourselves how long the breathing exercise should be performed until we feel in harmony.

All of the breathing exercises are very effective and should be performed in full awareness. These exercises promote our self-perception and are a tool that can help us find harmony and balance. With this tool, we can keep our overall system healthy and independent of others' energy. It thus preserves our independence, so we can become a source of energy for others, too, and not steal from others' energy systems.

Addict Behavior

Addicts will never tell us the truth. They lie because they always have to be right. They also do not consider themselves addicts. Therefore, they adapt everything around them to their own view of the world. They have a distorted truth. In one moment they argue 'this' and in the next it's 'that'. If it serves their truth, they will twist what was said in such a way that they can be right. For others, the whole thing is very confusing; they can never find out what the truth really is, because it does not exist. Addicts live in the moment. For them there is no truth. They live on their own level.

What is behind this behavior? The addiction makes them focus thoughts and actions on the addictive object. Everything is designed so they can live their addiction. We can be addicted to many things. Depending on the severity of the addiction, our whole life becomes reduced to this addiction. Everything else disappears from view. We live for and through the addiction, become farther and farther removed from reality and our fellow beings. The source of happiness and what makes life worth living is no longer found in the Divine, but in the addiction. At first, the addiction gives us the feeling of Divine energy (happiness), without us having to do much. But over time, all that remains is the addictive element. The feelings of happiness make way for the negative side of addiction that destroys us over time. We are destroyed because our source is the addiction. It is not a real source, but just a replacement. Only the Divine source can supply us with long-term feelings of happiness and Divine energy. Many addicts are people in search of spiritually. But they confuse the drug-induced feeling of happiness with true divinity. Addiction has many facets. We can be addicted to alcohol, drugs, partners, work, weight loss, sexuality, and much more. It is important that we recognize this as only a substitute for the Divine bliss, distracting us from our path. The temptations are what we succumb to. In serious cases of, for example, addiction to alcohol and drugs, our lives ultimately become focused entirely on this addiction. Life's radius becomes small, and we lose sight of the essentials. Instead of paradise, we experience hell on earth. We are tied to a physical level, and can no longer elevate our spirit – which becomes very heavy over time – to the Divine level. Our senses become blunted because they are exhausted. To find our way out, we often need the help of a specialist and the willpower to really want to change. Even then, it is a difficult path that consumes much of the addict's energy and that of everyone involved. If we believe in the power of the Divine, it can help us overcome the addiction. Using methods that develop this Divine power in a real and lasting way inside of us, we can better recover form the addiction and discover the Divine within ourselves.

Recognizing What Is Right

How can we recognize what is right in a situation? When it is right, we feel more energy. There is an inner attraction. In many cases, events accumulate that show us the way. For example, if we want to go on vacation and are undecided on the destination, we meet people with precisely this question in their own minds. When there are several alternatives, we always feel more or less attracted to one of them. There comes a moment where everything points in one direction and we are focused on one thing only. It has, ultimately, nothing to do with willpower. We will also go on vacation with people who are appropriate for us. Perhaps sudden obstacles prevent the person we had planned on vacationing with from joining us. To become conscious, however, it is important that we go through life with awareness. The spiritual world supports us on our way. All we need to do is pay attention to the signs that keep pointing the way. In addition, we need to trust in the spiritual world and be devoted. We cannot always rely on our willpower; not everything is the way we want it to be. In general, other people also have their influence, and circumstances are involved in the situation. Let us recognize that not everything is meant to be for us, and that ultimately the right things happen in our lives to support us in our growth.

Advanced Consciousness

With a state of developed consciousness, over time we can choose for ourselves in which state of consciousness we want to be. Sometimes, however, it is important that we deal intensively with one thing. In such moments, we leave the choice of consciousness up to the Divine, and accept what it has to say and the process we have to go through. It is important to distinguish when such moments are present. Often, we are free to choose our spare time activities. We are no longer driven by our mind, which may continually claim its space in our consciousness without letting us come to rest. With advanced consciousness, we are also able to consciously turn off the mind, so that we can rest. This state of restfulness gives us the chance to recover, and to achieve the levels of being. The uncontrolled thought processing in our brain stops. We enter into the silence. We detach from the material world and journey into connection with everything. Then we feel the lightness of being. We can practice this with the following exercise:

We visualize our brain. Our consciousness is focused on the front part of the brain including the middle part between our eyebrows (the Third Eye, see also the chapter "Balancing the Energetic System"). We observe our thoughts like an outsider and let them drift by like clouds. At some point, there is a moment when they stop. If we are not experienced, it might take longer to reach this state. Sometimes we can reach this state very quickly. It is important to take your time and not to force things. With time it will become easier to enter this state. Then, concentrating on this front part of the brain will be enough to immediately turn off our minds and enter a space of emptiness, which connects our being with everything. At the same time, in this state we are open to the Divine, which can communicate much better with us when thoughts are empty. Let's enjoy this state, so that we can recover from daily life and consciously recharge our energies. Normally, we are able to recover in this way only during sleep. Now, we have another way of achieving this state, other than by sleeping.

Living in the Moment

If we can be in the moment, we are in the here and now. In this moment, we are neither in the past nor in the future, but in the so-called state of "being." It is a more alert and relaxed state. We disconnect from experiences and see everything in a new light. We can meet our fellow human beings without bias. This new engagement allows us to completely re-discover people. It also gives us the opportunity to become consciously aware of and release our stereotypical patterns towards these people. We also give ourselves permission to free ourselves of our patterns. But we can succeed only if we detach from expectations, and from the past and the future. Since we live in a world where everything is directed as much as possible toward the future, and lessons from the past are only consulted to make a reality check, we are tasked with opening ourselves to entirely new dimensions. In addition, we need to let go of our usual patterns for a moment and open ourselves to a new reality. This can be confusing for us because we are accustomed to perceiving our environment according to judgments we made in the past. It also requires some practice to really engage with a moment and allow nothing else to come in. Fear may also be triggered when unfamiliar feelings emerge. Only by being can we experience how our entire body, our mind, and our soul may truly relax and open up to ever new feelings and sensations. Let us be open to this exciting experiment.

For purposes of practice, we can first engage with a flower by intense observation, to perceive with all our senses its uniqueness. We will probably see the flower differently in every moment, and no flower will be the same as any other. This statement can be applied to everything in our surroundings. The similarity is that the entire universe has a beginning, a phase of growth and, after reaching the zenith, a time of decay, which for mankind is completed by death. We will go through different stations in life as human beings in the same way, and yet every moment is, in itself, new. Let us take on this experiment by always being open to new things in life in a non-judgmental way, thereby providing our outside world with the chance of presenting itself to us anew, without having to conform to a pattern. In these moments, we reach out to our fellow beings so we can discover a new part of who they are and allow familiar old patterns, which may have lost their validity long ago, to die. We can do the same for ourselves if we are able to discover and engage with the new things within us. In this way, we can confront ourselves with the process of death and creation already during life. We can recognize that we don't have to be afraid, and that being open to something new gives us the chance to once again reinvent our lives and ourselves. Sooner or later this will allow us to experience more happiness and to build trust in our life's path. We are given the chance over and over again for rebirth on a new level, and to shrug off like an old backpack things that no longer serve our development.

Expressing Desires

How can we change our life and get what we desire? The general principle is that our wishes are fulfilled if they serve our higher good. To attract our wishes, we begin with the question: how would I feel if I were, for example, successful? After the mental or vocal expression of our wish, we observe whether it makes us feel good, and we look at possible images that may appear in this context. It is important that we assume the role of observer. If we feel good, we are on the right path. We can repeat the expression of our desire as often as we want. This method does not tempt our subconscious to work against us. It thus does not lead to a countermovement that tries to prevent the old and the familiar from being released. We create optimal conditions by expressing our desires in this way, so that we can achieve the goal.

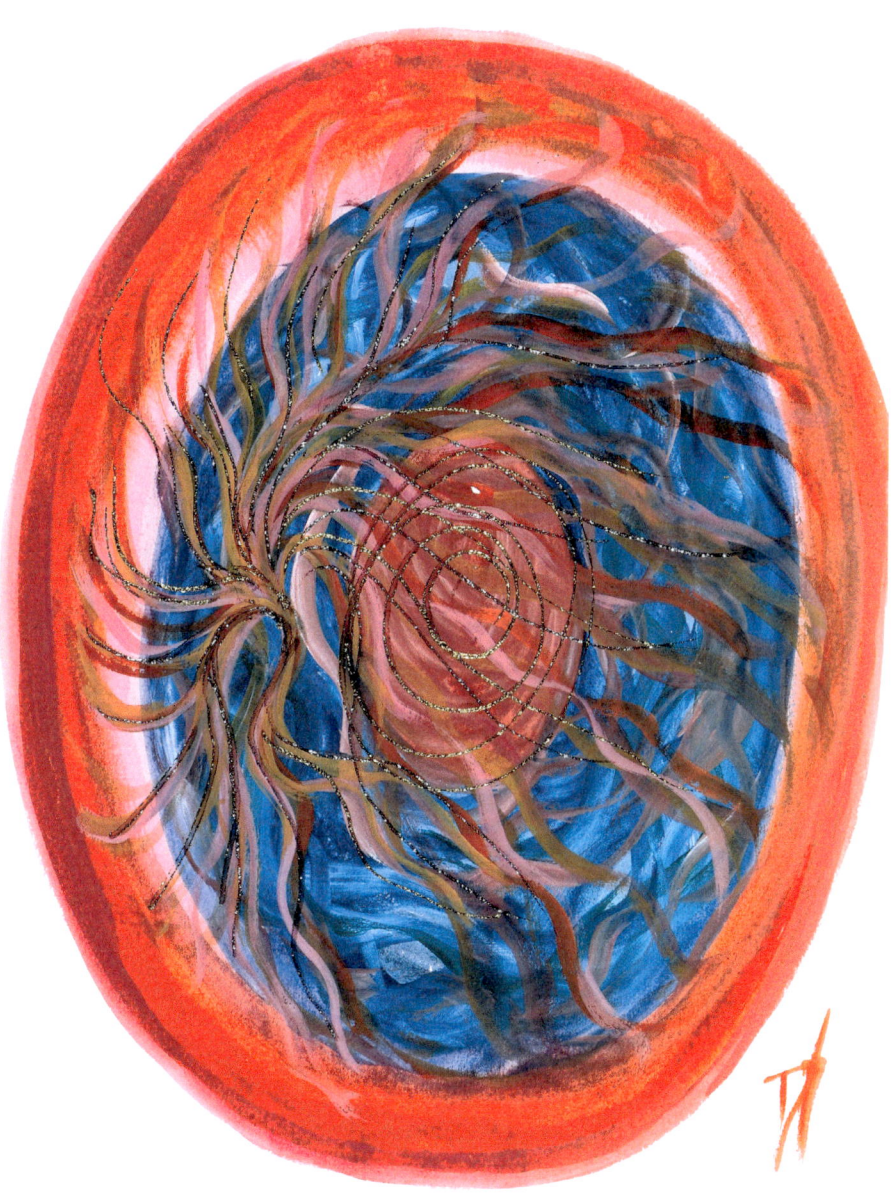

Integrating Energies

Sometimes we feel an urge within us, for example, to travel to another country. Do not hesitate to embark on the journey. Usually, there is an underlying desire of wanting to integrate a corresponding energy in connection with this country. This can also occur in connection with other endeavors. It is important that we give in to the urge if at all possible, so we won't stand in the way of our spiritual development, but instead support it.

Cleansing the Energy System

The following exercise should be performed to ensure that our energy centers are cleansed and we can capture more light:

We inhale light through our crown chakra and exhale it through all centers (third eye, throat, heart, navel, sacral and root chakra) (see also the chapter "Balancing the Energetic System"). We let everything that is clogged and heavy stream out of our centers together with light, so that we are freed from burden, and diseases stand no chance. We exhale in gradual steps, so that our whole body finally shines with light. We repeat this exercise until all heaviness has been breathed out of our bodies. We do this exercise for as long as we want. If we feel that the heaviness cannot be removed in one session, we will repeat the cleansing at a later time convenient for us.

Awakening the Third Eye

We ask our higher self to apply a spiritual tattoo in the form of a hexagon between the eyebrows at the location of the third eye (see the chapter "Balancing the Energetic System"). This tattoo is applied step by step: first, a blue triangle, tip pointing downwards, then a red triangle, tip pointing upwards, and finally a hexagon, which combines the feminine and masculine energies. The tattoo is to be applied until we feel that this hexagon on the third eye has been internalized. This hexagon can be used for visualization as well as for healing.

Healing

We inhale white light through our crown chakra, which we visualize as a star, and let it flow out from the center of the star. This protects us from tapping our own internal source of energy, and instead we use universal energy as the source (see also the chapter "Balancing the Energetic System").

For stronger healing, we ask our higher self to implement hexagonally shaped crystals on our chakras, with one corner pointing to the outside. This way, we can inhale bundled energy through the crown chakra and exhale white light step-wise through the individual chakras, starting with the Third Eye. Thus, the crystals can be used as lasers, which radiate energy like laser light. Depending on the intensity, the healing can be performed using white light, using silver light for potential intensification, and using golden light for even more intensification. White light should be used for the first treatment. Depending on the degree of perception, however, silver or gold can even be used the first time. This healing can be performed for ourselves or for others. For others, the chakras can be activated in series or used in another intuitive order.

Breathing Light and Color

When breathing light though the individual centers, depending on the effect of the absorbed energy, the crystals (see also the chapter "Healing") can be specifically enriched by the following colors in addition to the golden and silvery colors:

Red: for activating
Orange: for promoting a sense of security
Yellow: for strengthening the power of the intellect
Pink: for promoting the capacity for love
Green: for promoting creativity
Blue: for promoting calmness and connection with energy levels
Violet: for promoting spirituality

Once again, exhalation is step-wise, and can be used for oneself or for others. The more we practice the breathing, the easier it will become to intuitively use the color right for us. As a general rule, the colors are to be used according to their association with energy centers (see also the chapter "Balancing the Energetic System"). If colors cannot be clearly assigned, white is a safe choice because it contains all of the colors.

Trusting

Our faith that life is good and meaningful is continuously challenged. We encounter some adversity on our journey through life. What purpose is supposed to be served by losing our life partner or our job? The best we can hope for is that upon completion of one segment of any of our life situations, a new door will open. However, it is essential that we be able to open this new door trustingly. Everything in our life has its time. There are times of joy, worry, sadness, pain, etc. Let us give all these times their necessary space. Eventually, the moment will come in which we will look ahead with confidence and should re-open ourselves to life. Then life can bestow its gifts upon us once again for as long as we are open to them. We always have the choice of seeing the glass half full or half empty. It is up to us which spectacles we choose. Our life will be easier, however, if we see the glass as half full. Then we have a generally optimistic outlook, and therefore attract more things that are good. Let us make a habit of being thankful for the good things in our lives. We will be much more likely to succeed in leading a life filled with contentment and happiness. If we constantly focus on the things that are not perfect, we will become more and more dissatisfied over time, and our life will seem increasingly difficult. If we succeed in focusing the lens on the good, even in difficult situations in life, we will experience gratitude and more abundance in our lives. With a generally positive attitude, we will lead a fulfilling life and be a beacon of hope for our fellow human beings. Remember, it is easy to believe when circumstances are easy. It is more difficult to keep faith when life is troubled. This is when we are challenged to live our faith and grow with it.

Creating Energy

We can generate more energy in a targeted way with more people. Physically, we can accomplish this when several people are in one space, or when several people focus on the same thing over a distance. We are thereby able to create more energy than we could on our own. These energies can be used for spiritual work in a group or directed toward a greater goal. For example, everyone may focus on light and send it around the earth. It is important that the goal always serve the individual and the greater good. This kind of energy should never be used to the detriment of others; everything that consists of energy has an effect on the person who sent it, and therefore, ultimately, there would be a negative impact on the individual and the whole, because everything is interconnected. With group work, it is helpful if the individuals, if possible, sit in a circle and focus together on more energy, for spiritual work, for example.

Going into the Void

Sometimes there are very stressful things in life that we cannot ignore. However, it is not beneficial for us to deal with them constantly. Then we would always be burdened with this heavy energy and could no longer enter into a state of relaxation. Over time, we would feel drained and depleted of energy; all the more reason to step away from this stress every once in a while. When we go into the void, which means letting thoughts drift by and resting in nothingness, we experience select moments in which we feel free and can recover. All heaviness falls from us, and we enjoy resting in our spirit. We arrive at our innermost, can relax and allow ourselves to simply drift. As soon as we feel rested and strengthened once more, we can better handle the stresses in our lives. We can practice the following exercise (also see chapter: Advanced Consciousness):

We sit or lie down in a quiet place. Any position will work if you have experience. We observe our breath. Quietly, we breathe in and out. We let the thoughts drift by like clouds. We distance ourselves from everything and let thoughts pass by, should they arise again. With some practice, we will succeed better and more quickly at entering the phase of nothingness. At a certain point, thoughts no longer occur, and soothing emptiness spreads in us. We can relax and linger in this void, for as long as it is good for us. Then we slowly come back into our conscious mind and face the demands of life with renewed strength.

The Lightness of Being and Assuming Responsibility

Let us always consciously reenter this state of being. Let us try to accept life as it is, without worrying unnecessarily. We take action when it is our duty to do so. Let us be discerning, so we can recognize when we need to take action, or when it is someone else's job. The responsibility for our lives rests with us, just as the responsibility for other's lives rest with them. Let us not allow ourselves to be burdened and used by others so they can avoid their responsibility. The lightness of being gives us the opportunity to rest in between. We can let our souls wander. We feel this lightness whenever we consciously detach ourselves from daily life and retreat into being. We let go of all thoughts and surrender to being as described in the chapter: Going into the Void. If we assume responsibility for the lives of others – except for those of our children, where it is our duty – we prevent them from growing up. We impose a duty on ourselves and liberate others from theirs. We take on too much responsibility and they too little. They cannot grow, and ultimately develop a dependent relationship. There certainly are always exceptions where illness makes it impossible for people to make life choices on their own. But it is important to recognize when others are using us so they don't have to take responsibility for their lives. Ultimately we would assume responsibility for their lives, and would then also be responsible when things do not develop as desired in the lives of those people. Of course there are leadership situations in which we decide to assume a certain level of responsibility for others. But even when we adopt this leadership function, we are tasked with taking no more responsibility than necessary. It is important to look closely and – if necessary – to distance oneself. Let us recognize the things that need to be done, and then, in between, relax and recharge in the void. This way, we can always go back to our source, experience the needed relaxation in our lives, and draw new strength for our daily challenges.

Demons in the Form of Addictions

Low energy beings keep trying to gain power over us humans and reinforce their right to exist. The purer we keep our system, the less likely we may become a vessel for these energies. But any low vibration in us makes it more likely that we will be visited by these so-called demons. Let us take addiction as an example. The more we indulge ourselves and engage with the empty promise of heightened energies that are artificially triggered by addiction, the higher the price we pay. We become vessels for these energies, feel bad afterwards, and want to indulge once again in this intoxication, which, however, brings only brief relief. But the spiral is spinning ever faster and the pollution of our system offers more and more play for these low energy forms. They can only be kept alive by energy, which they need to do their mischief. We can obtain the highest form of protection by keeping our system as pure as possible and striving for true enlightenment. Addiction has many faces. Sometimes, it hides behind loved ones who try to ensnare us in their addiction. It is important to be aware of this and not become engaged with these negativities. If necessary, we also need to consciously retreat, and let the loved ones decide whether they want to remain prisoner of their addiction. Every person has a free will and has the right to decide how he wants to live. The primary relationship of addicts is with the addiction; they are no longer capable of truly entering a satisfying relationship having give and take. They are committed to their addiction and control their environment to satisfy it. Yet they will try everything, mostly in a highly manipulative way, to influence their environment in their favor. Let us be aware of this, so that we can see through this game and not further support the addiction or allow ourselves to be dragged into the abyss with them. If we are entangled in a situation like this, it also has a resonance within us. This needs to be examined, worked on, and released. Let us take a close look at ourselves and use the time and energy for us, so that we can attract healthy and constructive relationships. Otherwise, we attempt the impossible: leading a person out of an addiction he is perhaps not even willing to let go of. It is hard enough to change yourself. Therefore, we allow others to decide how they want to live. The best we can do is to decide whether we want to participate in or separate from unhealthy mechanisms. The decision is ours entirely. So let's decide and live with it.

Fate

The path of fate is sometimes unfathomable. Is there Fate or isn't there? Each of us can probably answer this question only for ourselves. Let us assume that there are no random encounters in our lives. Once we allow for this possibility, we can also see the messages that are behind the encounters. New opportunities can also be created that lead us on our way. Life has a larger meaning, we can perceive the signs on our way, recognize them with time as a signpost, and see that there are two sides to all situations in life. Nothing is entirely good or entirely bad. It is important that we engage with such events and are open to the deeper messages in life. This gives us the opportunity of going through life in a more relaxed and balanced state. We can recognize life's deeper patterns and interconnections and become more confident with this awareness. With time, we will become like weather-tested trees that will not as quickly be brought out of equilibrium.

Removing Blockages with Christ Energy

When we feel emotionally, mentally and or physically blocked, we can remove these blockages with the following exercise:

We sit or lie down and close our eyes. The concentration is on the root chakra, i.e. on the base of the spine. We visualize white energy and, based on the strength of its vibration, name it Christ energy. We feel this white and strong energy at the base and let it slowly rise along the entire spine while rising up the spine. We breathe completely calmly and relaxed while observing the sensations that ensue. If we feel that energy should linger for more time in one area, we allow it. When we reach the end of the spine, we continue with the neck and up to the crown. We do this exercise slowly and with concentration. When the exercise is completed, we remain lying for a moment and relax. As soon as we feel ready, we slowly stretch our limbs, open our eyes, and are once again fully in the here and now.

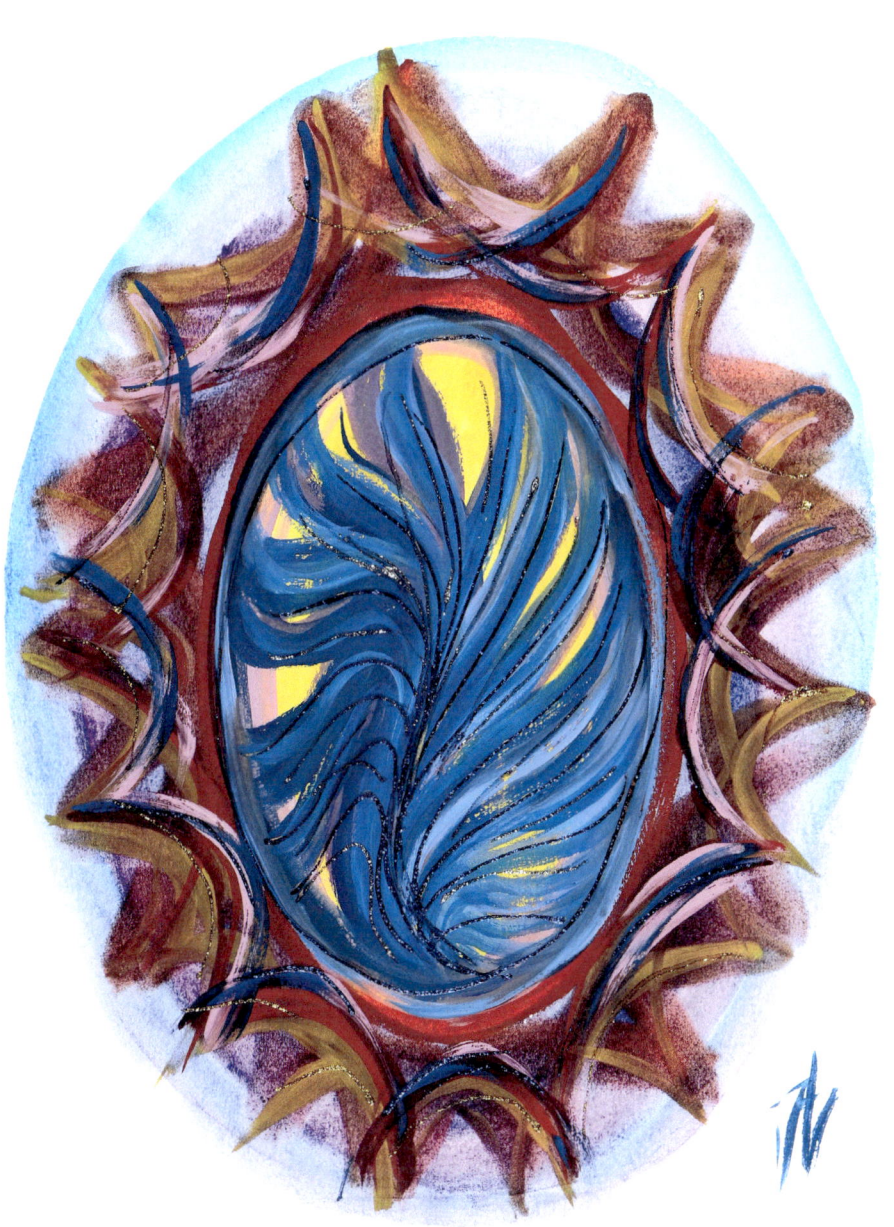

Keep Trusting

We are repeatedly asked to trust. Life does not always go according to our wishes. But we are always encouraged to make the most of it. It's easier for us if we can make sense of it. But most of the time, we recognize this only later, if at all. In general, we have no other choice than to accept what life has to offer in the moment. Sometimes we cannot change life despite our best efforts. Once we have done our best, we can trust that there is no more we could have done. Let us continue trusting that the outcome serves a purpose and ultimately advances us on our life path. With this attitude we establish basic trust in life and trustingly open ourselves to life over and over again.

Dark Times

We frequently experience times in which we feel life is a burden. We feel burdened from all sides. More and more stress is added. In times like these, we doubt that things will ever turn around. These are the dark times that usually precede times filled with light. In dark times we should continue to remind ourselves that light follows shadow, that we should not lose faith and that life represents change. In times like these, it is useful to take a closer look and perhaps take a different direction in life. We may have to draw within ourselves and take the time we need. Maybe parts within us still need refining before a new start can be attempted. We may also require the expertise from specialists and use it so we can understand certain situations better. It is also important that we do not rebel, but rather engage with this process that is apparently awaiting us in our lives. Here we are asked in particular to keep faith in the good sides of life and to take up the tasks we are challenged with. We cannot take on and carry the whole weight of the world on our shoulders. Let us trust in Divine providence, delegate the burdens, and strive to give our best anyway. Asking our higher self and God to give us the courage and the strength and to show us the way can help us not despair in this situation. Let us also try to feel that we are not alone. Let us trust that everything has a meaning that we will understand later, and let us thank the Divine powers for their support.

Interpreting Signs

At a certain point in our development we begin to receive more and more signs so that we can recognize the right path for us. We then have the task of interpreting these signs correctly. This is not always easy. We are therefore provided additional support to help identify the path we are destined for. But we also have the option of ignoring these signs. When these signs appear, we might first believe they are strange coincidences. But with time, we realize that there cannot be so many coincidences. If we are not sure what the signs want to show us, we can consult and communicate with our higher self. It should provide an answer in the form of inspiration. This may be direct (e.g., voices) or indirect (e.g., dreams, physical signals). We will keep receiving signs until we have understood the message that we are meant to recognize. It is important that we allow ourselves to engage on this level and be guided. This additional support in our lives lets us realize more and more that guidance exists, which we should gratefully accept. It helps us directly approach our mission in life, not get lost in the jungle of the physical world, and always stay in touch with the spiritual world. It also saves us from walking unnecessarily in circles in our lives, and helps us take on lessons we need to learn directly.

Trapped in Circumstances

There are certain situations in life we cannot easily bring to an end, despite our wanting to. For example, we may live in a relationship that to all appearances does not meet our needs. Or we may have an unsatisfactory job and yearn for something different. Despite all efforts, we are unable to change these situations. We apply for other jobs, but no other job is offered. We feel trapped in these situations. Even though we want to end the relationship, we are emotionally attached. Even after exhaustive efforts, no alternative appears. We can despair or give in to this fate and make the best of it. If we go by the law of resonance, we need to change before we attract something else. At such times, we are called upon to take the first step ourselves. If we change first, our environment will change too. Suddenly, there are other options on the outside, and we encounter different situations. Therefore, we are required to take that first step ourselves. In these situations, let us practice patience and not be too keen to rush forward. There are times when we have to tend to our own nature and something else must first mature. Then, with time, we can see that other options arise that are a better fit for our new personality.

Hopelessness

Sometimes, everything seems gray and black. We have no hope. Situations that we want to change persist, despite our best efforts. Everyday life is a battle. In moments like these, we are left only with the belief that some day things will be better, and that nothing lasts forever in life. Something is changing every moment. But we cannot always recognize it. Eventually, it will become evident through external events and also through changes on the physical plane. It is important in these situations of hopelessness that we don't stop making an effort to change. Sometimes it is not the right time to be active, but rather a time to go about our daily chores and to trust and pray that something will change. These phases are often preceded by something fundamentally new coming our way. We are in a state of confusion. The past is still there, but no longer to its full extent. It is about to fade, and the new has not yet arrived in our lives. Let us trust that this phase in our life will come to an end, and something new that is more aligned with our development will come into our lives. Let us persevere through uncertainty, and trust that the right thing is there for us at the right time. Let us not permit thoughts of doubt and confusion to hold us back too much, let's not try to force something to come into being that is still in the making and seemingly not ready for us yet – it has not yet come into our lives. Let us visualize what we want in our lives, pray that it will appear, and then let it go. In times like these, let us not focus too much on the confusion, but on the things around us that are filled with beauty and harmony, such as nature in her infinite beauty. Let us not quarrel too much with fate, but try to maintain a certain degree of calmness, so we can recognize when the time has come when we need to be active. It is sure to come.

Helping Others

Once we have found unwavering access to the spiritual levels, the suffering of others will not pull us down. We are able to stay in our frequency and offer real help to others. We can act as a bridge between heaven and earth. We make ourselves available as a channel. We also hold back on judgment. Our judgment disappears, and we begin to accept people as they are. Our ego is no longer involved. This condition allows clear and healing energy to flow through us that we can make available to our fellow beings, so they won't sink into the severity of the physical world and can have a glimpse of something greater than what can be perceived with the physical body. As long as we struggle with our own ego, the full healing power cannot flow through us, and at times we will be pulled down once again. Let go of everything and open ourselves trustingly to the spiritual world; then we can become Beings of Light more and more. Our field of influence will grow, and we can let more light flow through us and make it available to those in need. Our mind fades slowly into the background, and perception – which accelerates our spiritual growth – takes its place. We will walk in the light more often and feel lighter and more energetic.

The Art of Living

Loving what we have, rather than what we do not have, is an art. If we always focus on what we don't have, we are unhappy. And yet we need a vision of how things could be. The trick is to not let our visions spoil the present and enjoy what we have. Let us be grateful for anything that life has to offer in the moment, and let's keep our focus on our goals. Even though we sometimes try to change something, we still cannot. It is not the right time and nothing can be done other than accepting it. These conditions must be taken as given, and yet we must wait for the right moment to take action. The moment we accept this, we can continue to work on our vision, refine it within, and be clear about what we want in the future, so that we can continue our development. This is the art of living. This balance makes it possible to not always be unhappy and, at the same time, to not lose sight of our vision. To live the moment and not to think: how would it be if …? We let many moments pass by in our lives and don't make the best of them because our thoughts are somewhere in the past or the future. The only thing that counts is the moment in which we can live something physically. Ultimately, it is our decision what we achieve in our prevailing circumstances, and whether we are happy with it or not.

Being in the Flow

If life doesn't develop the way we imagine, we tend to put up resistance against it. We argue with fate and are no longer in the flow. This causes us to cut ourselves off from the source of vital energy and swim against the stream of life. Sometimes, we cannot understand why life hasn't turned out the way we wanted. We are hurt and sad. The faster we can come to terms with a situation and take a positive position, the better. Perhaps at a later time we will see the reason why something happened and can understand the purpose from a broader perspective. But at the moment when it happens, we are often left with no other choice than to let go and open up again to the stream of life, letting new things into our lives by accepting the given. The sooner we are able to do that, the better for our salvation and ourselves. Otherwise, we may become trapped in an energy blockage and may not be open to life developing.

Love Comes, Love Goes

Love comes and love goes. We cannot magically make it appear, and we cannot capture it. In the beginning, we are fascinated by love and want nothing more than having the loved one around us all the time. We see the person in the most beautiful colors. See the potential in them, until, over time, we recognize that not all that glitters is gold. Disillusionment spreads within us. Part of us feels betrayed and disappointed. Slowly, the paint chips off, and we see things that no longer fit our original image. We begin to adapt. But we cannot adapt indefinitely. If the distance between our wants and desires and reality is too great, love will crumble with time and become smaller. This process is sometimes painful and the initial bliss turns into suffering. We wrestle with ourselves and love and eventually the coin, which previously flipped to the side of love, now lands on the side of separation. The more often this image presents itself to us, the further we move away from love, and love from us. If this repeats over a longer stretch of time, the inevitable ending of the relationship looms ahead. Beauty has faded and all that remains is emptiness. At best, a friendship may develop from it later, which continues as a relationship between two people on a different level than on the love level. Then, the years of knowing each other and the intimacy can lead to something fruitful that can become timeless. We cannot determine when love comes and when love goes. The process of separation takes place before the end, and we may be able to influence that. It is wonderful if we can say goodbye at the end, grateful for the development that was permitted and for the learning on the love level with the loved one. Sometimes this is not possible, and we are filled with hatred and bitterness until we have processed the experience to some extent. These phases cannot be skipped, and we must live and process them.

Loving is always a small death of one's ego. When love finally leaves, a part of us dies that may have accompanied us for a long time. This causes suffering, especially if we did not consciously initiate the separation, or are the ones who were left. Suffering is part of being human, and has – like everything in life – a beginning and an end. It is analogous to developing and dying. Everything in life is part of this process, in the microcosm and the macrocosm. It is an ever-recurring process.

Trusting and Trusting Once More

Life challenges us in many ways. We are repeatedly challenged to open ourselves to life trustingly. Especially when life is not happening in line with our expectations, our trust in the goodness of life can be put to the test. If we succeed in seeing the good sides of life, we can look back on a happier life. The way we experience life depends largely on how we adapt to a situation. Even if we do not always succeed in wresting something positive from life, we can always try again. In many cases, we cannot easily change the circumstances. We can only change our attitude towards them. Let's engage with this work, and experience more and more happiness and lightness in our lives. We can practice this over and over with life situations. Don't let external circumstances always control our feelings and make us loose our balance. If we are peaceful inside, we will bring more calmness into our lives, and can relax more and more inside. From the position of peacefulness, we can better deal with difficult situations in our lives, and provide a place of tranquility, first for ourselves, and then for others. Ultimately, we recognize that the real being develops inside. This way, we can encounter outside storms with flexibility. Let's be flexible toward external circumstances, and move with the flow of time while being deeply rooted in our center. From this place of calmness we will become increasingly successful at calming the tides of the outside world and at attracting circumstances that are harmonious while radiating balance. As inside, so outside. Recognize life as a mirror of our souls, and swim with the tide and not against it. This helps us attain the greatest possible level of insight and self-development. Despite this, let us remember not to take everything, and ourselves, quite so seriously, to celebrate and laugh, too, and to live and exude the lightness of being.

Expanding Time

If we are able to live life in the moment, we can expand time. We suddenly have much more time on our hands. Things we had difficulty with, not having enough time, all of these problems disappear. We are able to focus all energy on the here and now. It's amazing how we can go through life much more relaxed and untroubled. We can even extend time in the moment it occurs so we can have even more time. We can achieve all of this by no longer holding ourselves up by judgment. Once we have removed resistance within ourselves, we let everything we encounter, and what life presents us with, flow though us. We are no longer slaves to our minds. For example, we no longer constrain ourselves by constantly asking ourselves what someone said and why it hurt us. These mind games take us out of the moment, and we lose energy for other things. This way we can better focus on what we really want in life. However, it is essential that we are open and accept everything without judgment.

How can we get into this flow of life? The fewer barbs we have within, i.e., patterns, the better we are able to step into the flow of life. These patterns resurface over and over again. We can observe them when we keep attracting people and situations that trigger these patterns. They show us where we have to work on. Let us be thankful to our surroundings for holding up this mirror. But we should no longer be slaves to our patterns. These patterns make us lose energy, which is then not available for us to handle the tasks at hand. Further, they always keep us either in the past or in the future. Then we are less balanced and unable to recognize when we become one with the present. The result is that we have less energy and are therefore not as happy and less balanced. So let us make use of all kinds of support tools that are offered to us, so that we come into this flow. The first step is resolving these patterns within us. As soon as they have been removed, we can feel more and more clearly how we are flowing with life. Let us also be thankful for always being able to recognize from the outside world what is within us. Let's start with non-judgment, and focus on our internal message. When we work on ourselves like this, we experience more joy and can better flow with life. Let us never forget: when we change ourselves, then our environment, which is our mirror, also changes. We can't change others anyway, and they will only hold on tighter to their issues when they feel we are pushing them. If we use this energy to make changes within ourselves, we will be rewarded with a more harmonious life flow.

Losing the Center

It may happen that we lose our center over and over again. Everything appears harmonious, and we are able to remain in this state for a longer period of time. Suddenly, events come up that throw us back; we are in disequilibrium and quarrel with fate. In these moments, it is important to hold on to inner harmony, to continue with our efforts to not stay in those disharmonious states of mind for too long, and to focus again on centering. We will find that this becomes easier with time. Don't resist life for too long when it wants to lead you in a different direction. Let us stop holding on to old things that are no longer aligned with our energy. Then we will feel more and more in the flow. The more necessary a change in our lives is, and the more we resist it, the more drastic our lives will force us into the new direction. Say yes to life, say yes to change. If we allow this, we will begin to resonate more and more with life, and start trusting that everything that happens in our development is for our own good. But we may recognize this only after the fact. For this reason, we must have trust, again and again.

The End of a Relationship

When is a relationship over? We wish sometimes we had a different partner. Still, we are not able to separate from the one we have now. We wonder why we cannot end it. Because most relationships contain an aspect of karma, we won't be able to end it before the karma has dissolved (law of cause and effect). At first, we will not understand. But we can assume that this invisible bond is showing us that we still have something to live and learn. Then, when the moment has come, we can separate from that person, or something from the outside world precipitates the separation. The ending of a relationship shows us that we can move on and – in the karmic sense – have fulfilled our calling. Sometimes, a partner will not let go, and, inevitably, this brings heartache. Let us trust in the higher powers, and leave it to them to show us the right way. Let us not resist too much, because something new is always waiting for us behind the old. A new life, which is better aligned with our present being. If we have trust in this consciousness, we can open ourselves and let go. We will be amazed to see what new things life will bring our way. Let us also have trust that we are always surrounded by circumstances that fit our needs. Let go!

Conclusion

The more we live in the flow of life, the happier we are. We no longer live only in patterns. The ego is not important anymore, and the Universal Laws can work through us. Living in the moment fills us with ecstatic joy, and life becomes more interesting and exciting. Everything in life is recognized and joyfully welcomed as a stage of development. Blockages are no longer triggered and therefore are not able to accumulate in the body. The body works as a resonance system through its energy points (chakras) and is in vibration with the outside world. An ecstatic dance results. The lightness of being and the art of living are attained. In this spirit, I wish all readers of this book the necessary insights and energy to achieve this goal.

List of Exercises

Living with Dark, Heavy Energies; Receiving Light 17
Spiritual Guidance; Making Contact 20
Heaviness in Body and Spirit;
Charging Energy and Light 30
Sexuality; Including Body, Mind and Heart 36
The Higher Self;
Balance between Activity and Passivity 58
Adopted Patterns; Resolving Patterns 89
Soaking up Life Energy; Increasing our Energy 92
Balancing the Energetic System; Harmony 94
Advanced Consciousness; Connecting with All 101
Living in the Moment; Opening Ourselves 104
Expressing Desires; Fulfillment of Wishes 106
Cleansing the Energy System;
Cleaning the Energy Centers 109
Awakening the Third Eye;
Connecting Female and Male Energies 110
Healing; Using Universal Energy 112
Breathing Light and Color: Targeted Development 113
Creating Energy; Combining Energy 118
Going into the Void; Resting in the Spirit 119
The Lightness of Being and Assuming Responsibility;
Letting Go 122
Removing Blockages with Christ Energy;
Releasing Blockages 127

List of Images

Receiving Light/Increasing Energy 13
Spiritual Guidance 19
Living Joy 23
Love 27
Sexuality 35
Guidance 41
Forgiveness 47
Perceiving Energies 51
The Higher Self 57
Trustingly Opening Oneself 63
Being Engaged 65
Recognizing the Right Path/Guidance 69
Present/Past/Future 73
Life 75
Perfection 79
Connecting to the Divine Level 83
Accepting 87
Soaking up Life Energy 91
Balancing the Energetic System 93
Recognizing What Is Right 99
Living in the Moment 103
Integrating Energies 107
Healing 111
Trusting 115
Creating Energy. 117
The Lightness of Being
and Assuming Responsibility 121
Fate 125
Keep Trusting 129
Interpreting Signs 133

The Art of Living 139
Trusting and Trusting Once More 145
Expanding Time 147

Glossary

For a better understanding, several terms that are mentioned often in the book are explained in more detail below:

Energy Centers (Chakras):

On a non-material level, our system is composed of energy. This energetic system contains various energy centers, also called chakras.

- **Root Chakra:**
This energy center is located at the base of the spine and is responsible for our physical sensations such as pleasure and pain, and for anchoring to the physical plane. The associated color is red.

- **Sacral Chakra:**
This energy center is located about a hand's width below the navel and speaks to our emotional life. The associated color is orange.

- **Solar Plexus Chakra:**
This energy center is located about a hand's width above the navel (solar plexus) and relates to the intellect. The associated color is yellow.

- **Heart Chakra:**
This energy center is located in the heart area and represents our ability to love. The associated color is pink.

- **Throat Chakra:**
This energy center is located in the throat area and speaks to the power of the word. The associated color is green.

- **Third Eye:**

This energy center is located between the eyebrows. It is responsible for perceiving the energetic level. The associated color is blue.

- **Crown Chakra:**

This energy center is located on the top of our head. It connects us to the spiritual level. The associated color is violet.

The pictures shown in this book and other pictures can be acquired from the author at the e-mail address dorisgraf_buch@hotmail.com.

The author

Doris Graf is a Master of Advanced Studies in Controlling with an executive MBA degree, a trained yoga teacher, and master astrologer. For many years she has held a senior corporate management position. Writing, spirituality and painting have accompanied her throughout her life. The connection of material employment with her engagement with spiritual levels generates synergies in Doris Graf. To her this means being connected on all levels, and at the same time, sharing a part of her innermost being.